SPOOKY
Wisconsin

SPOOKY
Wisconsin

Tales of Hauntings, Strange Happenings,
And Other Local Lore

RETOLD BY S. E. SCHLOSSER

ILLUSTRATIONS BY PAUL G. HOFFMAN

gpp

Guilford, Connecticut

Text design by Lisa Reneson

Illustrations and map border by Paul G. Hoffman

Map by Lisa Reneson © Morris Book Publishing, LLC

Library of Congress Cataloging-in-Publication Data
Schlosser, S. E.
   Spooky Wisconsin : tales of hauntings, strange happenings, and other local lore / retold by S. E. Schlosser ; illustrations by Paul G. Hoffman. — 1st ed.
       p. cm.
   ISBN-13: 978-0-7627-4562-3
   1. Folklore—Wisconsin. 2. Tales—Wisconsin. 3. Haunted places—Wisconsin. I. Hoffman, Paul G. ill. II. Title.
   GR110.W5S35 2008
   398.209775—dc22

                                                    2008008833

Printed in the United States of America

10 9 8 7 6 5 4 3 2 1

For my family: David, Dena, Tim, Arlene, Hannah, Emma, Nathan, Ben, Deb, Gabe, Clare, Jack, Chris, Karen, and Davey.

For Audrey, Carlos, Jack, Ashley, Diana, and everyone else who swapped stories and talked Wisconsin history and ghost-lore with a visiting folklorist.

And for John Russell, with my thanks.

* * *

Contents

PART TWO: POWERS OF DARKNESS AND LIGHT

SPOOKY SITES . . .

1. Milwaukee
2. Janesville
3. Buffalo County
4. Ridgeway
5. Madison
6. Prairie du Chien
7. Spooner
8. Baraboo
9. Portage
10. Apostle Islands
11. Vernon County
12. Peshtigo
13. Wausau

14. Mineral Point
15. Eau Claire
16. Green Bay
17. Douglas County
18. Mount Horeb
19. Sheboygan County
20. Spring Green
21. Green Bay
22. Rhinelander
23. The Dells
24. Ashland County
25. Door County

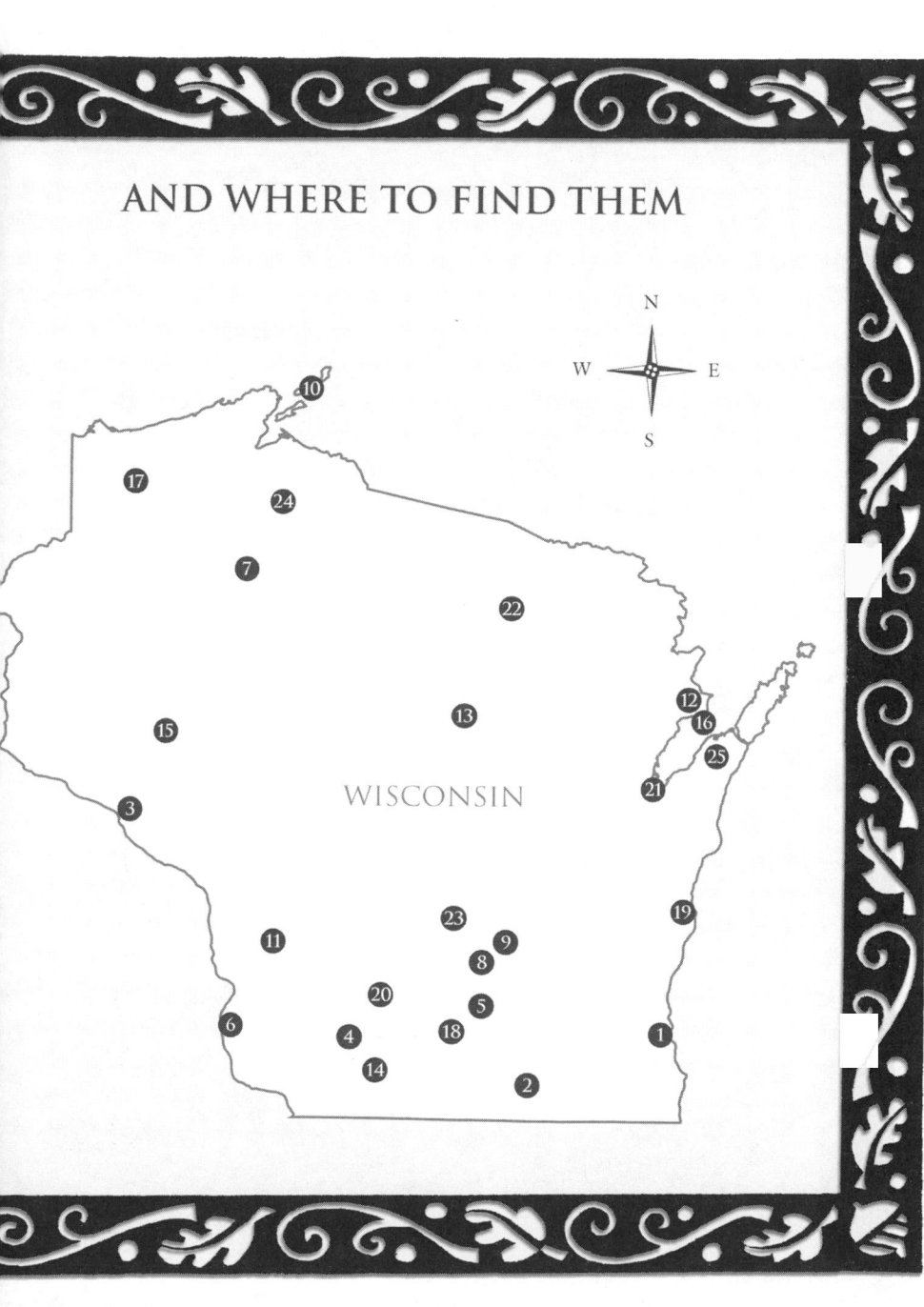

AND WHERE TO FIND THEM

WISCONSIN

Introduction

I was driving down Route 18/151 out of Madison when I saw a reference to the Grumpy Troll Brewery and Pub on a passing sign. My intended destination—that overcast morning of my third day in Wisconsin—was Mineral Point, but I found myself taking a right at the next exit. The Grumpy Troll? This I had to see!

I found myself driving into Mount Horeb—famed for its mustard museum, of all things. As the car climbed the small hill into town, I started seeing trolls all over Main Street. Wooden ones, I hasten to add—lest someone think I'd already had one too many at the pub! When I saw a sign for the Visitor's Center, I stopped to ask about the trolls, which I learned were made by a local artist. Enchanted by now, I wandered up and down the street to look at each one of them. Then I hit a bookshop and stocked up on books about troll folklore and bought a small replica of a troll to take home with me. (He's sitting next to my computer as I write this, contemplating mischief, no doubt, just like the *House-Troll* who met his end in Mount Horeb.)

After spending some time enjoying the Norwegian atmosphere of Mount Horeb and snapping photos of the six-foot Viking helmet on the wall of the building next to my car, I decided to keep driving down the road to the town of Blue Mounds (population 700) in hopes of finding a place to have some lunch. After wandering a bit, I found myself in a pleasant little pub with great hamburgers. I stood out like a sore thumb, of course, being the only nonlocal eating there. What fun!

Then I was off to visit the Cave of the Mounds, guided by a knowledgeable lady who showed me all of its delightful quirks, including "the Narrows," a passage almost too narrow to squeeze through; Polly the "parrot," a stalagmite that glows in the dark; a miniature cave inside a cave; a six-foot fossil in the ceiling of the cave; and black-and-blue stalactites. Outside again, I explored the grounds, which were fabulously landscaped with native prairie plants that climbed the hillside toward a red barn set at its peak.

Tired and hungry, I headed back to Madison, where I had dinner at a nice restaurant attached to the big West Towne Mall and learned some ghost stories from the waitstaff, Jack and Ashley. A swim in the hotel pool completed my day, and soon I was sound asleep, dreaming of mustard-eating trolls that strolled through caverns deep, talking to Polly the parrot. Another typical day in the life a folklorist.

I love Wisconsin. What a wonderful state! It is so rich in folklore and family stories that I could spend a lifetime there and barely scratch the surface. I filled my days riding through the rolling farmland, trying to imagine what it looked like when the primeval forest covered the land. I wandered north and south, east and west; from the Illinois border up toward

Lake Superior; from the Mississippi River across to Lake Michigan.

In Mineral Point, I visited Pendavaris, the site of a once-flourishing Cornish mining community. Parking in the shadow of the Merry Christmas Mine hill, I took a guided tour of the historic houses preserved by the museum and spent a delightful hour eating saffron cake (a Cornish favorite) and talking Tommyknockers and ghosts with the woman who ran the gift shop. As it turned out, she actually lived in an 1850s Cornish lead miner's house reputed to be haunted by a man in a black cape and top hat! Who knew a stop at the gift shop would turn up such a great ghost story?

In Schuylerville to the south, I once again entered the world of the Cornish miner and the *Knocker*, descending deep into a lead mine. (I entered via staircase, I hasten to add—no way would I have gone down via bucket, rope, and windlass like those intrepid miners did every day!) The mine ceilings were only four feet high in places, and mysterious passages veered this way and that. A cool spring bubbled up inside one passage, and the guide informed me that the miners had once stood in its chilly waters as they worked hour after hour, using only one candle at a time to help them locate and mine lead. Must have had eyes like a cat!

In Eau Claire, I visited the Paul Bunyan Logging Camp Museum to learn more about the life of the lumberjacks who once strip-cleared most of Wisconsin and to learn more about the massive folk-hero and Babe, his big blue ox. According to Paul Bunyan lore, the larger-than-life lumberjack spent one whole season in the woods of Wisconsin fighting the effects of the *Dark Lord's Curse* after inadvertently upsetting the Lake Superior water god known to friends and enemies alike as Matchi Manitou.

I could go on and on about my adventures in Wisconsin. In La Crosse I took a paddleboat ride on the Mississippi River, where *Whiskey Jack* once rode his rafts down to the lumber markets in Saint Louis. In Green Bay, I spent several peaceful hours walking the shores of Lake Michigan where the French-Canadian *voyageurs* once roamed, and Helene almost married a *loup-garou*. In Door County, I discovered a small-town

park right on Lake Michigan and sat on a wooden swing watching the approach of a huge storm that whipped the water into whitecaps and made the shore grass bend and wave in a mad fury. It reminded me of another fierce wind that once heralded the approach of a massive whirlpool, sprung miraculously to life in time to defeat a terrible enemy trying to invade Washington Island (*North*).

From Ringlingville, once home to the Ringling Brothers Circus in Baraboo, to Pepin, once home to Laura Ingalls Wilder; from the stately dignity of Madison to the bustling breweries and hubbub of Milwaukee, Wisconsin is a state brimming with history and lore. I spoke to people from all walks of life—mining experts, lumbermen, museum curators, shopkeepers, schoolchildren, eminent scholars, tourists, and fourth-generation residents—and gathered more spooky stories than I could ever write about. My favorites are in this collection.

It was with great reluctance that I bade farewell to the Badger State, and I've already got my next trip planned. If you happen to be in Madison come early summer, be sure to stop by for a chat. I'll be sitting on the terrace in back of the Union, looking out over Lake Mendota and eating homemade ice cream. See you there!

—S. E. Schlosser

PART ONE
Ghost Stories

1

The Shrouded Horseman

MILWAUKEE

When the Civil War ended, Jeremiah Jones, once a slave, found himself a free man. Eager to make a new life for himself, he made his way north to Milwaukee. For several years, he worked odd jobs until he earned enough money to buy himself a big white horse and a dray—a low, flatbed wagon without sides. Shortly thereafter, he was hired on as a drayman with the Phillip Best Brewing Company.

Jeremiah had carefully studied each of the breweries in town and had decided he wanted to work for the Bests. The company had a good reputation. It was started by a German family who came to Milwaukee in 1842. At first, they had opened up a vinegar works. Then Father Best, who was a brewer, arrived from Mettenheim, and the family decided to set up a brewery instead. They bought a place on Chestnut Street Hill, and young Phillip contracted with a local ironmonger to build them a boiler. When it was ready, Philip walked down the hill carrying his entire fortune tied up in a red handkerchief. He gave it to the ironmonger as a down payment for the boiler, and when the kindly man allowed him to take the boiler immediately, he promised to keep the ironmonger swimming in beer for the rest of his life. Kept his word too; that ironmonger never wanted for drink another day in his life. Lived eighty years, too!

At first, the Bests did all the work themselves in the brewery, even the making of barrels. Then business started to boom, and they were forced to hire on more staff, especially after they took sides in a political debate about the new state constitution. The Bests supported a provision on suffrage for the city's foreign-born people, and Francis Neukirch, a competitor in the brewing industry, opposed it. The Bests' stance on the issue created a movement among city's immigrants; suddenly, they started boycotting the "anticonstitution" Neukirch beer and encouraging all and sundry to drink the "proconstitution" Best beer. Proconstitution supporters would line up on one end of the bar, taunting the other side by toasting "Prosit, Best," while the anticonstitution contingent countered by shouting "Prosit, Neukirch" from the other side. The shrewd tavern keepers claimed they could serve either Best's or Neukirch's beer to their customers, but the fact was that all the beer was drawn from the same keg!

The Best family business prospered as a result of the feud, so much so that one of the brothers left the family enterprise in 1848 to start a brewery of his own, which he later sold to Miller for $10,000. Meantime, the prospering family brewery was renamed the Phillip Best Brewing Company when son Phillip took control of the business in 1860. Two of Phillip's son-in-laws were responsible for the management of the brewery, and it became the first exporter of Milwaukee beer.

A major turning point for the Best brewery came in the fall of 1871 when much of Chicago burned down, including most of that city's breweries. Best, along with Miller, Schlitz, Blatz, and others, were quick to fill Chicago's gap. By 1872, half of Milwaukee's beer was sold out of town. The city's population was only seventy-five thousand, but Milwaukee's breweries shipped more beer than did New York, Philadelphia, or St. Louis. By this time, Best was the leading Milwaukee brewery. In 1869, the company had produced fewer than twenty-four thousand barrels. By the time Jeremiah Jones joined the company in 1873, it was turning out one hundred thousand barrels annually—more than any other American brewery.

Jeremiah would begin each day by stopping his dray wagon in front of the stone-lined hillside vaults that resembled caverns, where the kegs of beer were chilled. Once his wagon was loaded, he would begin his delivery rounds, greeting everyone with a cheerful smile and a joke that delighted the brewery's customers and earned him a good reputation among the Best management staff. He was so industrious and trustworthy that he was given more responsibilities and better pay. Jeremiah quickly earned enough to buy property on the outskirts of town. He built a beautiful little cottage and a big barn for his white horse and dray.

Once he was settled into a home of his own, Jeremiah decided it was time to marry. He had his eye on a pretty girl named Lucille whom he had met while out on his deliveries. Whenever duties permitted, he'd park his dray near Lucille's house, and the two lovebirds would laugh and talk together. Sometimes they'd walk shyly along the road, and he'd give her wildflowers he'd brought from his cottage garden.

No one in Lucille's family considered the relationship more than a casual friendship, so they were taken completely aback the day that Lucille came into her home and announced that she and Jeremiah had just been married by the justice of the peace.

Her parents were surprised by the match but quickly resigned themselves to the situation, not wishing to alienate their only daughter. But for Lucille's brother James, it was another matter entirely. He thought that Lucille had married beneath her, and he hated the former slave for stealing his sister's heart. James was so enraged that the drayman had presumed to marry his only sister that he turned bright red and couldn't speak for a full five minutes after Lucille broke the news.

Then he grabbed Jeremiah by the collar and kicked him roughly out of the house, using the most offensive language imaginable. Jeremiah did not dignify the foul words with a response, but Lucille, watching, knew that he would not soon forget his new brother-in-law's treatment.

James followed Lucille up to her room and begged her to have the marriage annulled. Ignoring him, she calmly packed her bags—tossing them out of the window to her new husband when James blocked the door—and then climbed out the self-same window herself and down the wisteria vines to the grass below.

Lucille left her parent's home forever in the dray drawn by the large white horse, and she never set foot in that part of the city again. She and Jeremiah lived simply but happily in their little cottage by the woods. Lucille's mother sometimes stopped by to visit and would spend the day sewing with her daughter and chattering about their friends and neighbors. Nothing was ever said about James, who had loudly disowned Lucille the day she left home to marry Jeremiah.

Three months had thus passed when Lucille returned home from a Ladies Aid meeting early one evening to find an empty house. This was strange. Jeremiah was usually done with the chores by now and sitting at the fireside intently reading the daily newspaper. She glanced around the small cottage, puzzled by his absence. Grabbing up a lantern, she went out to the barn.

As Lucille approached the wide double doors, her heart started pounding in fear. There was an oddly metallic smell in the air—the smell of blood. Something was wrong! Lucille wrenched the barn doors open and stepped inside. The light of the lantern fell onto a blood-stained floor. Then she saw the broken body of her husband lying a few feet away. With a scream of terror, Lucille ran to him and knelt down in a puddle of blood.

"Jeremiah," she cried. "Jeremiah!" There was no response. She hadn't really expected one. There was so much blood all over the floor. No one could have lost so much and still be alive.

Time had slowed down for Lucille. Each second ticked by like an age as she placed the lantern with exaggerated care on the floor beside her husband's body, reached out with shaking hands, and turned him over. His face was battered almost beyond recognition; his arms and legs broken in several places. Half-hidden under his leg she saw a familiar silver pocket watch—one that she had last seen attached to the waistcoat of her brother James.

"Oh, Jeremiah," Lucille sobbed, pulling his bloodied body into her arms and rocking back and forth in agony. "Oh, my love."

Her screams had alerted their neighbors, Charlie and Jane, who came running to find out what was wrong. Charlie took one look at the mess inside the barn and immediately sent his wife home. He tried to get Lucille to get up and go with his wife, but she didn't even seem to notice he was there. She just kept sobbing as she clutched her husband's body in her arms.

It was a long time before Charlie could persuade Lucille to lay the body down. He helped her gently to her feet, and she watched dully as her neighbor covered Jeremiah with a thick horse blanket. Then he escorted her firmly back to the cottage and asked his wife to minister to the stricken woman.

Walking grimly back to the barn, Charlie went to check on the white horse and was not surprised to find it lying dead with its throat cut. A few feet further on, Jeremiah's dray lay smashed to pieces. Charlie shut the barn doors carefully on the scene and went to summon the sheriff.

Lucille's brother had fled the city by the time the sheriff arrived at his house to question him regarding the murder of Jeremiah Jones. A warrant was put out for his arrest, but James was nowhere to be found. After the funeral, Lucille put the cottage up for sale and went to live with an aunt in Madison, unable to bear the thought of staying in the city where she had lost her husband so cruelly. No one in the area wanted to buy the house, thinking it had been tainted by such a brutal murder, so it remained empty. Charlie and his wife looked after it for Lucille whenever they had time to spare. And that was that. Everyone thought this particular story had ended, and life in Milwaukee went on as usual. Until one evening at dusk, when the phantom appeared.

It was Charlie who saw first saw the ghost. As he rode his horse into the barnyard early one evening, the animal suddenly reared with a terrified whinny. Charlie was almost thrown. He wrestled for control and finally managed to bring the horse back down on all fours. Only then did he look up and see the dray drawn by a glowing white horse coming slowly down the road. It was driven by a tall figure wearing a gray shroud that whipped and flapped under the force of an invisible gale. The wheels of the dray were a good two feet above the surface of the road. It took all of Charlie's strength to keep his terrified horse from bolting as the phantom drayman turned down the lane toward the Jones place and passed out of sight. Charlie had recognized the horse and dray at once. The spirit of Jeremiah Jones had returned a month to the day after he had been killed.

Sightings of the ghost became frequent in that section of Milwaukee. It was not uncommon for fellows to stagger into the local tavern, white as a sheet, and collapse at the bar for a few drinks after seeing the shrouded figure driving toward them with its robes flapping in the unearthly wind. There was something menacing about the phantom, which drove all the highways and byways, as if it were seeking something . . . or someone. Charlie was convinced that Jones had returned to avenge himself upon his murderer and would not rest until he found him.

About six months after the sightings began, Charlie was summoned to his front door one evening at dusk by a harsh knocking. His wife looked up in alarm, and Charlie motioned for her to stay in the kitchen as he went to open the door. Standing on the porch was a drunken, red-faced figure that he recognized at once as Lucille's brother, James.

"Where's Lucy?" the man slurred, looming over Charlie until their noses almost touched. "I looked for her on the farm, but she ain't there. Where's she?"

"Lucille has gone away," Charlie said, motioning to his wife behind him with one hand. *Go get the sheriff,* he willed mentally to her. *Go get the sheriff.* He heard the back door click softly and knew she was on her way. Now all he had to do was keep James occupied until the sheriff arrived.

"We've been taking care of the cottage for her," he said, trying not to breathe in the alcoholic fumes that were wafting off the tall, swaying figure. "Would you like to see it?"

THE SHROUDED HORSEMAN

"My cottage now," slurred the elder brother. "I earned it!" He chuckled to himself, obviously delighted by the crime he had committed against his sister and her husband.

Charlie led him off the porch and walked very slowly across the farmyard to give his wife time to run down the road to the sheriff's place, which was a half-mile away. Lucille's brother wasn't in good shape for walking, anyway. He staggered this way and that, first bumped into the fence and then tripped over the front gate. As Charlie stepped out into the road, a cool breeze unrolled over the landscape like a frozen carpet. Charlie gasped, his eyes fixed on a point of blue light down the road.

"Whatcha stopping for?" grumbled James, righting himself and giving the gate a vicious kick for good measure. Charlie didn't answer. He couldn't speak. Always before, when he'd seen the phantom, it had been calmly driving along in its dray. But tonight, the dray was careening down the road with the shrouded figure standing up in its seat, cracking his long whip ferociously. The white horse was wild-eyed with fury. It picked up speed when it saw the man who had killed it and its master, and it gave a scream of anger that turned Lucille's brother around in his tracks.

With great presence of mind—considering the circumstances—Charlie stepped back behind his fence, leaving Lucille's brother to face the music alone. The drunken man stared at the glowing figures pounding toward him down the road. He swayed left. He swayed right. He stumbled backward, trying to find his feet. On the fourth try, he managed to sort out left leg from right and fled with a scream that was all the more terrified for its delay in coming to his throat. He scuttled down the road, weaving back and forth, with the drayman and his horse thundering at his heels, the horse snapping at his back and the glowing whip cracking across his shoulders. Charlie watched them until they disappeared out of sight.

A few minutes later, Jane came racing home, her blue eyes huge with amazement and fear. "Did you see?" she gasped. "Did you see?"

"I saw Jeremiah chasing that no-good brother of Lucille's down the road," Charlie said.

Jane nodded vigorously. "The phantom got him just as the sheriff and I came out his front door. The ghost snapped the end of the whip around his leg and pulled him off his feet. Then the horse and dray drove right through him! James gave a sort of gasp and then flopped onto the ground, dead as a mackerel, with a look of sheer terror on his face. And serves him right too," she added. "Nasty, horrible man. Justifiable homicide by a ghost, the sheriff called it. I'm going inside right away to write and tell Lucy."

She marched into the house, and Charlie followed her, after sending one more incredulous glance down the road to the place the phantom had appeared. He had a feeling that this was the last time they would ever see the ghost of Jeremiah Jones—and he was right.

2

Practical Joker

When Old Man Thompson died of natural causes in his sleep, folks about town heaved a quiet sigh of relief. It wasn't that we'd hated ol' Jed. It was because we'd no longer have to suffer any more of his dad-blame practical jokes, which had annoyed many of us for years.

Jed's escapades were legendary. There was the time he loosened two wheels on Missus Lawrence's wagon while she was waiting at the train station to pick up her new mother-in-law. The wheels fell off as they drove out of the station yard, and the elder Missus Lawrence went crashing over the rail of the bridge and into the stream below. The Lawrences were still not speaking to Jed twenty years later, long after old Missus Lawrence had gone on to Glory herself.

Then there was the summer Jed milked the Frederickson's cow dry every afternoon. When his task was complete, Jed would leave the milk in very strange places: up a tree, down by the creek, in Missus Frederickson's sewing room. Once he even left it under the bed! The Fredericksons began to think that an old-world hobgoblin had followed them when they had emigrated from Cornwall. But one day Mr. Frederickson came home early with a toothache and caught Jed in the barn.

That Jed! I could tell tales of him for days. He'd leap down on people from the branches of tall trees. He'd come running out of nowhere and jump on the tongue of a passing wagon, scaring the horses half to death and sending them careening down the road. A couple of times he leapt into the driver's seat of a wagon, tossed the driver over the side, and raced the horses around and around town before abandoning the wagon several miles from the driver's original destination.

And on my farm, he'd once appeared dressed like a cowboy and leapt atop old Bessy the cow like she was a horse. He cracked his whip, yelled at the other cows, and "rounded them up." Of course, what he really did was cause a stampede. I chased him off my property waving a burning-hot branding iron in my fist, and that was the only practical joke Jed ever played on me. He claimed I had no sense of humor.

The whole town turned out for old Jed's funeral. Some were truly sorry to see him go. Others—like the Lawrences—were there to make sure that Jed wasn't joking this time. "Wouldn't put it past him to come leaping out of his coffin in the middle of the service," Mr. Frederickson said dryly to me as we sat down together in the same church pew at the funeral. We kept a close eye on the casket from the first prayer to the final amen, but Jed stayed where he was and didn't even pop out when they lowered the casket into the ground. So that was that.

About a week later, Bart Bailey—the town drunk—came staggering into my yard at dusk. He was shaking from head to toe and as pale as if he'd seen a ghost. And that's just what he claimed. Said Old Man Thompson had jumped down on top of

PRACTICAL JOKER

him from a tree branch and had ridden him from the abandoned mill to the head of my lane before dropping off. The missus and me put it down to alcohol, of course—Bart Bailey was rarely sober—but truth be told, I didn't actually smell any alcohol on Bailey's breath that evening.

I found out two days later that Bailey had been telling the truth. I was in the small cheese factory behind our barn, pressing cheese curds into molds, when I heard my cows stampeding all over the pasture. I raced outside to see ol' Jed in his cowboy costume cracking a whip over the heads of my panicking cattle as he rode poor Bessy around and around the field. Jed was whooping and hollering and waving his whip above his head. His body was glowing with bright white-blue light, and you could see Bessy's back through his ghostly legs. Bessy herself was wild-eyed with fear. She snorted and quivered as she raced along the fence, trying in vain to dislodge the terrible creature on her back.

"Jed, you get down this instant before you kill that cow," I roared, leaping over the fence in one furious bound and racing after the phantom cowpoke and his steed. Jed laughed and laughed. He pushed Bessy another few paces before he leapt off her back. Bessy kept going after the fleeing herd. As I watched, they burst through the fence, trampling the wood into tiny splinters, and headed toward the back fields and the big cow pond. "Now look what you've done," I shouted at the ghost, who was shaking with laughter. "Who's going to fix that fence?"

Jed grinned, pointed a finger at me, and then vanished with a popping noise like a cork coming out of a bottle. "That's what you think!" I shouted up toward the sky in the off-chance that the good Lord had actually allowed Jed into Heaven—though I had my doubts.

The cows wouldn't come near the front pasture for a week after that, which was good since it took me that long to fix the dad-blame fence. At church on Sunday, I told Jed's eldest son that if his father's ghost ever came to my house to play cowboy again, *he* was going to fix the fence. Jim Thompson nodded glumly. He was in no position to disbelieve my story. Reports of the ghost's antics had been coming in all week long. Yes, there was no doubt in anyone's mind that old Jed was back and worse than ever.

Jed's ghost took to haunting the main road out of town. Folks never knew if they were going to reach the general store in safety, or if the ghost was going to jump onto the tongue of their wagon and spook their horses so severely that they careened madly through the town and ran for miles out into farmland on the other side. A number of the local ladies started walking to town. A few tried riding their horses, but old Jed would occasionally drop from the tree branches right behind them and ride pillion right past the general store, cackling as the frightened horse bolted for the horizon.

The wheels on the Lawrences' carriage came off with such regularity after the return of the ghost that they were forced to check each one before leaving the house on errands. Mr. Lawrence went so far as to insist that Jim Thompson's wife had to drive Missus Lawrence whenever she wanted to go to town to shop or attend the weekly Ladies Aid meetings to make sure she wasn't left stranded on the side of the road. This meant an additional six-mile round trip for Jim's wife and a whole day wasted whenever Missus Lawrence wanted to do errands. Naturally, this made Missus Thompson angry at the ghost of her father-in-law, and she started making Jim's life pretty miserable as a result.

It was the day that Mr. Frederickson found his cow milked dry and the bucket of milk stranded on the roof of his house that things came to a head. Frederickson came galloping into town on his horse, pop-eyed with rage at the ghost who had been making all of us miserable for the past two months. He leapt off his foaming steed, threw the reins to the innkeeper's young son, and raced down the road usually haunted by ol' Jed, waving his fists and shouting in rage. Naturally, those of us in town doing errands dropped everything to follow him. It being a Saturday, that was just about everyone—including the Lawrence family, me, my missus, Jim Thompson, and his wife, too.

"Get out here, you no-good wiseacre, and take it like a man," Frederickson howled dementedly up into the trees. "I can wrestle you from here to kingdom come, and by golly, I will! I'll learn ya!"

"A wrestling match! What fun!" The ghost of Old Man Thompson jumped down from a tree branch behind Frederickson and tapped him on the shoulder. Frederickson whirled and leapt upon the ghost with a growl that sounded more like that of a bear than a human.

The crowd stood back as man and ghost wrestled back and forth across the dirt road, their arms and heads locked together. Frederickson managed to get a throw on ol' Jed, but the ghost just flipped about in midair and floated back toward his adversary.

"Unfair use of phantom techniques," shouted Mr. Lawrence, dancing up and down in rage. "Point goes to Frederickson!"

The crowd was definitely on Frederickson's side, including Jed's son and daughter-in-law. I'm not sure exactly how long the match lasted, but finally Frederickson collapsed to the ground in sheer exhaustion, clutching at his heart. Jed floated a few inches above him, hands clasped in victory above his head. And that's when his daughter-in-law struck.

"Fa-THER!" she screamed like a banshee. Jed whirled around in alarm and held out his hands pleadingly. But Missus Thompson had had enough. She advanced like an avenging angel upon the ghost as a couple of us pulled poor, exhausted Frederickson out of the way. "You've destroyed property, ruined perfectly good horses and cattle, and plagued the life out of everybody in town!" she shouted. Behind her, her husband found his tongue and began shouting himself in a neat counterpoint to his wife. The two Thompsons corralled their erring parent against a large tree trunk and scolded and railed and roared at him so loud that I might have felt sorry for the ghost, if I hadn't remembered old Bessy, who still refused to come out of her stall in the barn. That was enough for me. I joined the Thompsons under the tree, shouting my own complaints, and the rest of the crowd followed suit.

The ghost of ol' Jed stared frantically from his furious children to his furious friends and neighbors. Everyone hated him! "I was just having some fun," he explained, his glowing back pressed defensively against the bark of the tree.

"Fun!" howled his daughter-in-law. "You get back to heaven right this minute and stay there! Or I'll get the preacher to exorcise you. See if I don't!"

Jim nodded in grim agreement, and ragged cheers arose from the crowd surrounding the tree.

"Oh, alright. None of you has any sense of humor whatsoever," the ghost grumbled as he started to fade out. "You never did."

"Just go!" Jed's daughter-in-law commanded.

"I'm going," said ol' Jed, and he disappeared with a loud, final pop.

"Good riddance," said Frederickson weakly, speaking for us all.

"And don't you come back!" shouted Missus Thompson, waving her fist into the air on the off-chance that the good Lord had actually allowed her erring father-in-law into heaven, which most of us doubted.

That was the last we saw of ol' Jed Thompson. But I have no doubt that he's still around, playing practical jokes on the angels in Heaven (or maybe on the denizens of a hotter region) at every opportunity.

3

Unexpected Guest

There! He heard it again. The soft thud-thud of muffled footsteps carried faintly through the midnight darkness and falling snow. Someone was following him.

He quickened his pace, pulse beating madly in his throat. He attempted a few surreptitious looks over his shoulder but saw nothing except swirling snow. But he could feel the other person's presence distinctly, and it made him nervous.

He moved quickly past the silent houses, aiming for his own home at the edge of town. His stride was as long as he could make it without turning it into a run. His mind was already racing. Why would someone follow him home from Christmas Eve service? Was it a thief, hoping he carried extra money in his wallet on this festive occasion? Or an unknown adversary? His pulse gave a painful throb at the thought, and he cursed himself for not carrying a weapon, or even a cane. But who thought of needing a weapon on Christmas?

He might be safe if he made it home ahead of his follower, though the house would be empty of all save his elderly housekeeper, sleeping in her small room on the top floor. Briefly, he regretted being an elderly bachelor who had never considered marriage. But that decision had been made long ago.

He was starting to tire as he turned into his street, fumbling under his cloak for the house key in his waistcoat pocket. His long fingers were trembling with cold though his body was sweating with strain, and his legs were hot and trembling from the unusual pace he was setting through the swirling snow. And then he realized that he could no longer hear footsteps behind him. He slowed his pace a fraction, listening hard, but there was only the soft frizzling sound of snowflakes hitting the houses and the streets.

Had his unknown follower managed to get in front of him, he wondered, picking up the pace again? Or had the footsteps just been those of a parishioner on his way home? The snow became heavier, driving against his face, his cloak. He had neglected to wear his hat this evening and regretted it now as he hurried up the stone steps leading to his front door. He turned the key in the lock and glanced back down the snow-filled street. There was nothing there, no footprints save his own. As the lock clicked open, he noticed that his arm was strangely free of snow. In fact, no snow clung to either hair or garments, though he had distinctly felt its coldness as it drove against him on the journey home.

Shaken by this strangeness, he leapt into the safety of his home and slammed the door shut against the memory of the frightening walk. But he couldn't block out the other odd circumstance. He touched his dry hair, where no hat had sat to shield it from the swirling snow. He touched his dry cloak, which should have been soaked through during the long walk through the storm. A single snowflake melted against his questing fingers and was gone. It was as if he had walked home in a bubble that had kept the falling snow away from him.

He was panting with superstitious fear as he took off the dry cloak and hung it on the coat rack by the door. Based on the condition of his clothes, one might be pardoned for thinking that he'd taken a stroll through a midsummer's night rather than a midwinter snowstorm.

A cold breeze seemed to sweep through the house, and he shivered and rubbed his arms as he mounted the staircase to the library. His housekeeper had kindled a fire for him before he left for the midnight service, and the room should be cozy and warm by now. He desperately needed the warmth after the strange occurrences of the past half hour.

As he hurried into the library, a man's voice called his name. He blinked in astonishment, and then a huge smile lit his face. Sitting in a chair beside the blazing fire was Andrew—the old friend and daring companion of his youth! Andrew had long ago moved to Washington, D.C., to take a position in the federal government, and the occasional letter was all he had heard of his friend during the years that followed the move. Yet now Andrew was here, sitting in the old chair by the fire that he had always favored when he had visited in the past.

"Andrew! What are you doing here, you old rascal?" he exclaimed.

The superstitious dread and apprehension he had felt during his strange walk home vanished unnoticed as Andrew leapt to his feet in welcome. The two men shook hands vigorously and clapped one another on the back. He noticed that his friend's hands and body were icy cold, and he quickly urged Andrew back to his seat by the fire.

"So you sweet-talked my housekeeper into letting you in, eh, old chum?" he asked jovially, not waiting for an answer. "What brings you to Wisconsin during this merry holiday season? I thought you were permanently ensconced in Washington."

"I had a yearning to spend one last holiday with my old friend," Andrew said with a smile.

"And it's splendid that you're here! I was thinking on my way to midnight service that it would be a little lonely celebrating Christmas by myself," he said. "But come, tell me how things have been with you?"

Andrew was glad to tell. The old men chattered back and forth merrily, interrupting each other again and again as one happy memory was jogged by another. He hadn't felt so elated in years as he did at this moment, sitting by the fireside with his old friend in the chair opposite him. Finally, he realized that he was being a poor host.

"Why, Andrew, I've kept you here chatting and not even offered you food or drink!" he exclaimed. "Didn't my housekeeper give you anything? Never mind," he finished without waiting for his guest to respond. "I'll run to the kitchen and fetch us a snack. Want to come along?"

Andrew shook his head. "I'll stay here by the warm fire," he replied. "Perhaps we can eat here? I'm still a bit chilled from my walk here this evening."

Remembering how cold his friend had felt when they shook hands, he nodded. He hurried to the kitchen and slapped together a cold supper, grabbing the first couple of plates he could find. They were mismatched—one with blue roses and one with yellow—but Andrew wouldn't care. Then he poured a couple of tankards of ale and brought the whole kit and caboodle back to the fire.

They chatted merrily all through their late-night supper. It wasn't until he sat back in his chair, replete and contented, that his gaze fell upon the mantel clock and he realized how late it was.

"Why Andrew, I've kept you up half the night! How rude of me, when you've journeyed so far. Come, I'll put you in my best guest room, and we can chat again in the morning! My housekeeper makes an excellent breakfast, and Christmas dinner will be something to talk about for years to come!" He pulled his guest out of his chair and escorted him upstairs to the guest chambers.

"We'll talk more in the morning," he said again, as he showed his visitor upstairs. Andrew smiled a little sadly and did not respond. He just stepped through the door and bade his host goodnight.

He returned to the master bedroom, which was on the same floor as the library. When he got to bed, he slept heavily but not well. He tossed and turned in his sleep, reliving the terrifying moments when he thought he was being followed home over and over again in his dreams. It was the sharp voice of his housekeeper announcing the imminent arrival of breakfast that finally pulled him from his bed, tousle-haired and red-eyed with fatigue.

"I'd better wake Andrew," he muttered sleepily, pulling on his dressing gown inside out and putting each of his slippers on the opposite foot. After nearly tripping himself, he put his slippers on the correct way and struggled with the sash of his robe as he headed for the stairs toward the guest room. He'd just discovered that the sash was inside out because his robe was inside out when he caught a glimpse of the scene inside the library on the way past the door.

UNEXPECTED GUEST

He stopped abruptly in astonishment. There, on the table where he'd left them, were the plates and cups they'd used the night before; but one plate was still heaped with drying, cold food, and one cup was full of untouched ale. He walked slowly into the study, staring at the untouched plate. It had yellow roses around the edges; the plate Andrew had used. He'd seen Andrew eating off that very plate last night around two o'clock in the morning and drinking ale from the mug beside it. He'd seen Andrew putting the empty plate on the table right where it was sitting now. *Hadn't he?*

Turning on his heel, he raced through the door and upstairs, the ends of his untied robe flapping about like a shroud in a high wind. He knocked briskly on the guest room door and then entered without waiting for a reply. "Breakfast, old man," he said in a forced-jolly tone. The room was empty, the bed smooth and covered with a light sheen of dust. Obviously, no one had slept in this room for months.

"Andrew must have been upset about the service after all," he said uncertainly, staring blankly into the empty room. "I hope he didn't stomp off in a rage. Or perhaps he was ill?" The knot in the pit of his stomach that had formed at the sight of the untouched food grew larger.

Ignoring his suddenly shivering body and the chills running up and down his spine, he ran downstairs to the kitchen and asked his housekeeper if she'd seen Andrew that morning. The housekeeper's answer was short and to the point. She'd neither seen nor heard anyone arrive last night, nor anyone leave this morning. And she'd not stepped one toe inside the guest room. If there were to be two to breakfast, she wished her employer would see fit to tell her so immediately. If not, then she'd thank her employer if he would get out of the kitchen and let her finish her work. He backed out of the kitchen apologetically, saying that there would be "just one for breakfast" after all.

He stood in the hallway nervously trying to thrust his hands into the inside-out pockets of his robe. Why had Andrew left without saying goodbye? Why was the plate with yellow roses still heaped with food? *Why had Andrew bothered coming at all?*

The mystery disturbed him, and he spent a restless Christmas Day wandering about the house, picking things up and putting them down again absently as he tried to understand what had happened the previous night. He nearly terminally insulted his housekeeper by picking absently at his most excellent Christmas dinner, and he finally fell asleep in the library in the chair that his old friend had—or hadn't—occupied last night.

He awoke late the next morning, his neck stiff and sore from lying in the chair, to the sound of the front door briskly closing. He rose and tried to stretch out the kinks in his body, then headed out the door toward the stairs. His housekeeper met him at the top step with the morning mail on a silver tray.

"Here are your letters, sir," she said, handing the mail to him. She tutted disapprovingly when she saw his rumpled, slept-in clothes. "I'll get your breakfast," she said briskly.

He hardly noticed her departure as he glanced through the letters in his hand: A bill, an advertising circular, and a letter in an unknown handwriting. He opened the letter first. It was from Andrew's daughter in Washington, D.C. Her message was short and to the point: "It is with great regret that our family wishes to make known the death of our father Andrew to all his old friends and colleagues." There was a bit more to the letter, but his mind couldn't take it in. Andrew was dead? Then who . . . how?

He sank down onto the top step, his body trembling. The letter dropped from his shaking hand and drifted to the floor below as his mind slowly put the puzzle pieces together: The sound of footsteps in the snow; the strange dryness of his clothes; the chilly old friend who was reluctant to leave the fire; the full plate; the empty bedroom. The answer was obvious, really.

He had spent Christmas Eve with a ghost.

4

The Brothers' Revenge

RIDGEWAY

A foul blizzard raged that night long ago when the forest grew tall and thick and the farms were few and far between. A wayside inn could mean the difference between life and death to a weary traveler on such a night. And so it was with life-saving gratitude that the two waifs stumbling through the swirling snow spotted the tall bulk of the saloon and pushed their way through the door.

They were young men—boys really—two brothers with dark hair and blue eyes, and faces made red and sore by the driving snow, which stung like buckshot against their skin. Every eye in the saloon turned upon them as they awkwardly brushed encrusted snow from their jackets and made their way to the huge fireplace. The bartender frowned sourly, watching the hot fire steam their garments dry. Such young lads probably had little money to pay for food, drink, or lodging.

"That fire's not free," he called to the lads. "Buy something or out you go!"

A few minutes of intense whispering between the boys produced an order for coffee and some coins to pay for it. Satisfied, the bartender went to fetch the hot drink, leaving the lads to the merciless stare of the regular customers. After a moment's study, most of the regulars returned to their conversations, ignoring the newcomers. All save for one massive man: a butcher with a mop of red hair and a long red beard who was the worse for drink. He glared at the boys as they slipped out of their damp coats and sipped at the hot coffee. Finally, the little brother's nerve broke, and he spoke to the man. "What do you want, mister?"

"You're looking at me funny," the butcher slurred. He rose slowly, growing taller and taller until he loomed over the two boys. "I don't like funny looks."

"We weren't looking at you in particular," said the older boy, placing himself in front of his younger brother. "We were just looking around the room while we warmed ourselves by the fire."

The butcher's face contorted. "Are you calling me particular?" he shouted. Around the room, the scarred, rough-looking crowd grinned. This was a tough saloon, and its regulars dearly loved a good fight.

"Peculiar is more like it," called a man from a nearby table.

The butcher swayed, his reddened eyes narrowing as he looked around for the source of the voice.

"We didn't say that," said the older boy quickly, waving his hands for emphasis. One of them struck the butcher on the arm. That did it.

The butcher whirled like a cat in spite of his inebriated condition and grabbed the elder brother by the collar. "No one hits me and gets away with it," he roared and threw the boy headfirst into the huge fire raging in the hearth.

There was a moment of stunned silence in the saloon, and then the elder boy screamed in agony as the flames engulfed him from head to toe, the hot fire quickly igniting his hair and woolen garments. The younger lad shouted in terror and leapt forward to rescue his brother. The older boy stumbled out of the fireplace, head and body aflame. The little brother tried to beat out the fire with his small hands as the elder brother screamed in anguish, face and body already burnt beyond recognition by the consuming flames.

"Help me! Get some water!" the younger brother shouted to the occupants of the room, blue eyes blazing with panic.

The butcher loomed above them, grinning sadistically at the burning figure that had sagged to its knees, screams dying away as the boy lost consciousness.

"Now *he's* warm enough," the butcher said. "So it's your turn."

As he reached for the collar of the younger boy's ragged collar, the bartender came running up with a bucket of water and threw it on the burning figure.

"Leave the boy alone!" he shouted to the butcher, but the little brother had already struggled free and fled for his life out the door of the saloon into the raging storm, leaving behind his coat, which lay drying on a chair by the fireplace.

"Someone go get that lad before he freezes to death," snapped the bartender, stooping to smother the older boy's still-smoldering garments with the blanket he'd tossed over his shoulder. It quickly became obvious that his efforts to save the elder brother were in vain. The boy was dead.

By the time he looked up from his grisly task, the butcher was gone and the occupants of the saloon had vanished, apparently not wishing to be linked to a murder. Covering the boy's body with the blanket, the bartender threw on his coat and went looking for the other lad in the howling snowstorm,

THE BROTHERS' REVENGE

but to no avail. The boy's little frozen body was not found until the spring, buried in a snowdrift near the crossroads.

It was not long after this that the hauntings began. A black spectral dog would appear on the crossroads at night, harassing all who passed that way. A mysterious light would blink on and off over the place where the younger brother had lain buried for so many months. And sometimes, when the moon was full, a burning figure would run screaming through the fields. Folks were afraid to travel the road at night for fear of what might follow them home.

One evening, a decade after the death of the two young boys, a burly man with a long red beard came strolling down the Ridgeway road. He had not been seen in town since the double murder, but so much time had elapsed that he had decided it was again safe to enter the town he had once called home. The butcher whistled to himself cheerfully as he walked down the moonlit road. He'd heard rumors of a ghost but had discarded them as so much poppycock and tavern talk.

As he meandered down the road, he became aware that a silence had fallen. The crickets had ceased to chirp, owls had quieted their hooting, and even the wind had died away. In the odd silence, he heard a soft padding sound, like the footsteps of a large animal. They walked when he walked and stopped when he stopped. The butcher became aware of a blue light that slowly lit up the road from behind him, and he realized that he could see his shadow wavering strangely at his feet. Pulse pounding madly in his wrist and chest, the butcher turned. Behind him, large as an ox, stood a black dog with blazing blue eyes and sharp teeth. The butcher had seen those blue eyes once before, gazing at him from the face of a young boy trying to save his burning brother.

The black dog growled softly, a sound that sent shivers down the back of the massive butcher's spine and froze his legs. "It wasn't me that done it," he said, shivering from head to toe. "You've made a mistake. It wasn't me."

The dog took a step forward, and the movement unfroze the butcher's legs. He whirled around to flee and found himself face to face with an impossibly tall figure covered from head to toe in flames. The burning boy reached out toward the butcher with hands withered and blackened by fire. His legs were just stumps with little flames whipping up and down where his feet should be.

The butcher gave a terrified scream and fell, blood gushing from eyes and nose. He was dead before he hit the ground.

Folks thought that the butcher's death would have ended the hauntings at the crossroads, but the black dog and the flaming figure still appeared from time to time to harass travelers and speed them on their way. Perhaps the brothers' spirits still resented those men who watched the butcher abuse them without lifting a hand to help. Perhaps they just didn't know how to break free from this world.

Whatever the reason, the Ridgeway phantoms remained in the vicinity until 1910, when most of Ridgeway—including the saloon where the boys were so monstrously abused—was destroyed by a fire. It is said that the angry faces of two blue-eyes boys appeared amidst the flames as the town burned to ash around them, but no one knows if this is the truth or just a rumor. Whatever the case, the fact remains that after the fire, the phantom brothers were never seen again.

5

The Cabinet of Skulls

There was a young fellow living in Madison way back in the early days who fancied himself a bit of an anthropologist. He was fascinated by the animal-shaped mounds left by the Mound Builders all around Wisconsin and did some digging whenever he had free time from his job at the Dry Goods and Grocery, where he worked as a clerk. He excavated all sorts of mounds—bird-shaped mounds, turtle mounds, panther mounds, and even a bear mound or two. At first the young chap was pretty excited—expecting all sorts of treasure to be buried in the mounds. But all he found were the remains of the folks who were buried there more than a thousand years ago by their families. Interesting from a historical point of view, but not from a financial one. Still, he carefully recorded where he found each of the skeletons, placed the bones into wooden boxes, and put the skulls into an old display cabinet that he kept in the garret of the big house he'd inherited from his folks.

After a year of two of digging in the mounds, the young feller met a pretty girl and courted her good and proper, with flowery speeches, long drives in his buggy, and Sunday school picnics. He married her a short while later, and—following a brief honeymoon—brought her home to the big old house with the cabinet full of skulls in the garret.

Well, the first morning they were home, the chap's little wife took it into her head to clean her new home from top to bottom. A few minutes after she entered the garret, she came screaming down the stairs in hysterics because a skull had knocked her in the head when she'd opened the door of the display cabinet. The young fellow explained to his lady that he'd been doing some anthropological research on the mounds, but that explanation didn't placate her. She wasn't happy about having all those skulls in her home, and she even accused her new husband of defiling the sacred mounds and behaving in a sacrilegious manner toward the dead. All of which was probably true, and her husband might have agreed—except that her cross attitude and angry demand that he rebury the poor skeletons turned the young fellow stubborn. He refused to get rid of his skeletons and told his wife that if she didn't like them, she shouldn't clean the garret anymore.

And that was that. The wife refused to set foot on the staircase or even go near that part of the house, and the husband refused to rebury the skeletons. They agreed to disagree, and there the matter stood until later that night, when the couple was awakened by the pounding of a ceremonial Indian drum and the shuffling of many feet in the garret overhead. The sound of the drum was accompanied by the soft chanting of many voices and the occasional sobbing of some grief-stricken soul. The introduction of a new person into the household, in combination with the disturbance of the skulls in the cabinet, had apparently awakened the spirits bound to the bones in the garret.

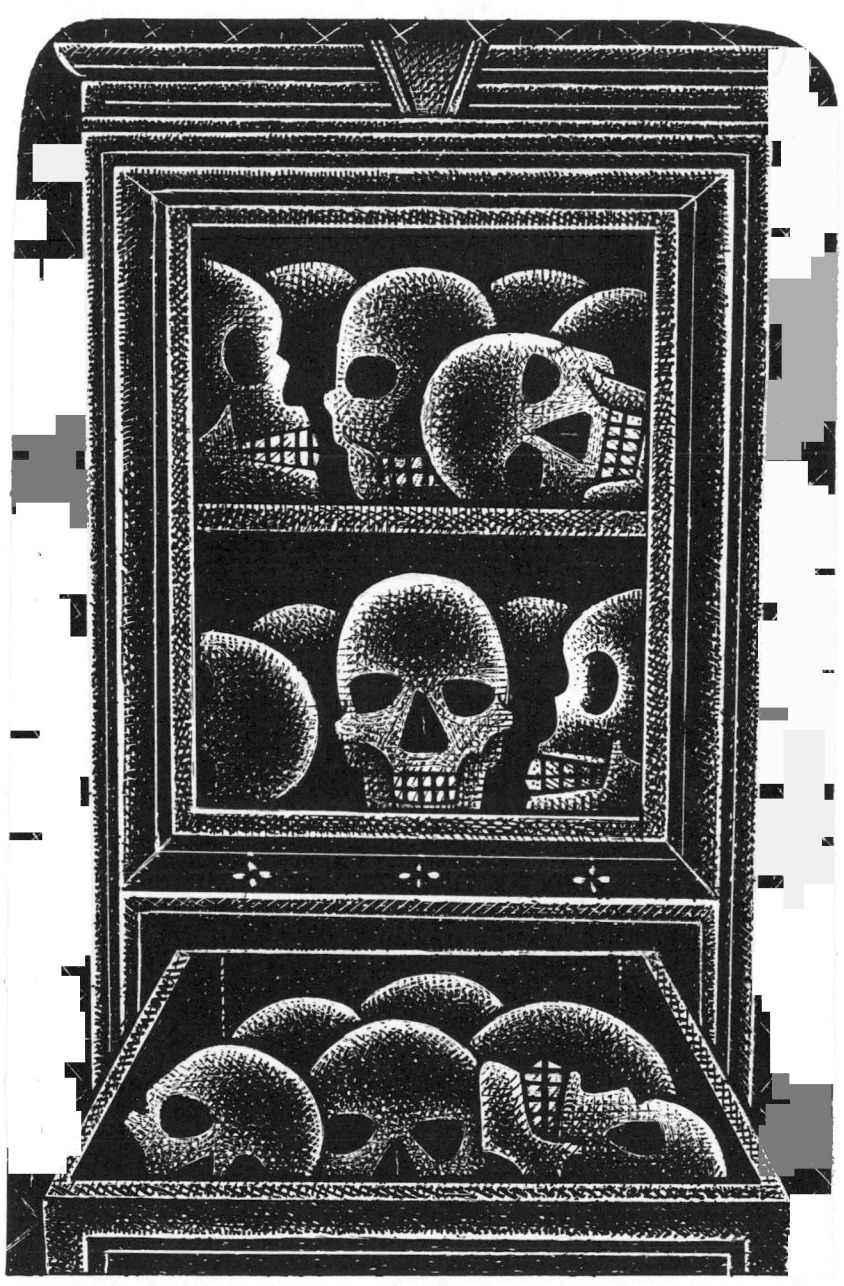

THE CABINET OF SKULLS

This ghostly performance was too much for the little wife. With a shriek that could wake the dead (those that weren't already dancing, that is), she leapt out of bed and threatened to leave her husband if he didn't get rid of the skeletons in the attic. Unnerved by the ghostly noises coming from the garret, he agreed to take the skeletons to the local historical society the very next morning.

As soon as it was light, the young fellow put the boxes of bones into a handcart and piled the skulls willy-nilly into a big old basket. Then he wheeled the cart into town, stopping only once at the top of a small incline to take a drink from the flask of water he carried with him. As he paused, he heard the sound of two little girls coming up the hill behind him. He turned to look at them, listening as they argued with each other about the existence of ghosts. He grinned to himself, wishing they could have heard the phantom drumming coming from his garret the night before.

"My Pa says there's no such thing as ghosts," the little blond-haired girl said impatiently, stamping her foot.

"Is too! My big brother's seen them floating in the woods just after dark," said a small girl with brown braids and a gap in her teeth.

"Prove it!" said the little blond girl.

It was at that moment that the basket of skulls, perched precariously on the back of the cart, tumbled off and rolled down the incline toward the two little girls.

The little blond girl's mouth dropped open in astonishment. Then she gave a shriek of terror and fled back down the road with her friend at her heels, crying: "Ghosts! The ghosts have come to get me!"

The girls disappeared around the bend in record time, leaving the young husband to trudge down the hill, collect his skulls, and carry them back up to the handcart, laughing the whole way. That little encounter almost—but not quite—made up for his having to give up his anthropological hobby in favor of domestic happiness.

The historical society was delighted to accept the carefully documented remains of the Mound Builders, and they were put on display with other artifacts of the period. And if the night watchman ever heard the sound of phantom drumming and the shuffle of many dancing feet after the arrival of the bones, he never told anyone.

But the young man never excavated a mound again.

6

Whiskey Jack and the Haunted Island

Back in the days when the forests of Wisconsin were thick and deep, and lumberjacks ruled the northern shores, sawmills processed thousands and thousands of pine logs that had to be taken downriver. Shipments of lumber were made up into huge rafts that were rowed with sweep oars down the Wisconsin and Mississippi rivers all the way to Saint Louis and beyond. The rafts were so large that they could carry a pilot, a shanty with a stove and a cook to prepare meals, plus many raftsmen to steer and row the cumbersome load downriver.

It was a tricky run, and many men lost their lives navigating the rapids, river crossings, snags, and sandbars. When raftsmen hit a wide sandbar or shallow water, they would have to unhitch the sections of raft and carry them across one at a time and then spend hours in the water rehitching the sections for the continued journey. At night, they would tie up the raft to the riverbank and sing ballads and tell stories. Sometimes they would go into the local towns to drink or attend events.

These raftsmen were mighty men, strong and agile. But none more so than Whiskey Jack. Standing seven feet tall in his stocking feet, Whiskey Jack could best any man in a brawl, drink any man under the table and still be stone sober, and overcome any obstacle on the river. Men queued up when they heard Whiskey Jack was going to be the pilot of a lumber raft. He always got his rafts in ahead of schedule, sometimes earning the crew a bonus; he hired the best cooks in Wisconsin to feed his men; and he never missed an entertainment upon the river.

One time, when Whiskey Jack heard that the circus was playing in town, he tied his lumber raft up for the night in a fairly deep side stream and took the whole crew to the big top to watch the event. Just then a twister sideswiped the town, knocking over the tent and scaring all the elephants away. When Whiskey Jack and his raftsmen returned to the stream, they found all the elephants wallowing in the water next to the raft. By then, those critters had drunk so much water that the raft was sitting on a sandbar and had to be taken apart by hand and hauled to deeper water in the morning before they could depart. But Whiskey Jack still finished the run in record time by rigging a huge sail to the center of the raft and letting the wind blow it down to Saint Louis jiggedy-jig!

Another time, when the raft cook ran out of meat halfway through the journey, Whiskey Jack took his rifle and went deer hunting. Right quick, he found himself face to face with a big, mean old bear, and no shots left in his muzzle loader. So he clubbed the bear on the nose and then went running back toward the raft, figuring that his men could shoot the bear for him. As he passed the raftsmen lounging on shore, he shouted: "I got me a bear and I'm bringing him back alive!" Well, those men jumped in the water right quick and swam for the raft—even those who knew only how to dog paddle. If it wasn't for the presence of mind of the cook, who took out his rifle and shot the bear clean through the head, the boys would have had to eat beans for supper.

Once, when funds were low and the men were thirsty, Whiskey Jack went into the local saloon and offered the bartender a bundle of lathes—thin strips of metal that could be nailed in rows to framing supports—in exchange for a drink. When he finished his whiskey, the bartender told him to set the bundle of lathes outside by the back door. No sooner had the back door swung shut on Whiskey Jack when another member of his crew came in with a bundle of lathes to swap for a drink. This went on all evening until the entire crew had drunk their fill. It wasn't until after closing time, when the bartender went to look out the back door at the huge pile of lathes he thought he'd been collecting that he realized the whole crew had traded him the same bundle over and over again!

Oh, the stories about Whiskey Jack were legend on the Mississippi. But there was one tale about the pilot that he disliked intensely, and no one dared whisper it when he was anywhere about for fear that he would clobber their lights out. That was the story of the haunted island where the mighty raftsman was rousted by a ghost.

It seems that one of the islands in the Mississippi had the reputation of being a sacred place to one of the local tribes, and a curse was said to come upon anyone who violated that sacred ground. River pilots avoided the spot, and there were rumors spread by raftsmen, pleasure boaters, and steamboat captains claiming that flickering lights and ghostly figures could be seen

WHISKEY JACK AND THE HAUNTED ISLAND

on her shores after sundown. No one lived on the island, and no raftsman would tie up on her shore, even though it was prime anchorage for that spot on the river.

Well, Whiskey Jack had heard all the tales about the haunted island, and he thought they were nonsense. He'd never seen anything but trees the many times he'd rafted past, and he didn't believe in ghosts anyhow. So at dusk one spring evening when Whiskey Jack found himself on that stretch of river, he gave orders to his men to tie up the raft on the bank of the haunted island.

The men went pale with fright when they heard the order. Finally, the cook spoke up. "We shouldn't tie up there, boss!" he exclaimed. "That island is haunted. We'll be swallowed whole by the ghosts."

"I ain't afraid of no ghosts," Whiskey Jack snapped. "Don't be questioning my orders. If we see any ghosts, I'll lick 'em with both hands tied behind my back!"

One look at Whiskey Jack's face persuaded the men to row for the haunted island. Better uncertain death by ghost than a certain beating by the massive river pilot, was the consensus. When the raft was secure, Whiskey Jack went ashore. After a moment, he realized that he was all alone on the bank. Every man jack was still on the raft, and no matter how he cussed and shouted, none of them would set foot on the island. They would sleep on the raft instead.

"Lily-livered cowards, the lot of ya!" Whiskey Jack shouted, and he took himself to a soft spot on the moss to sleep.

It was a peaceful night, with crickets chirping and owls hooting and the river swishing and chattering softly to itself. Whiskey Jack was soothed to sleep by the familiar noises. It was around midnight that the night sounds ceased abruptly and the air on the haunted island grew cold. Whiskey Jack shivered and reached for a blanket, which he'd left in his pack on the raft. Snapping awake, Whiskey Jack cursed himself for leaving it behind.

At that moment, the ground underneath him began to throb softly, as if to the beat of a giant heart. Small white lights like candles popped up on all sides of the island, and the murmuring of many spirit voices could be heard. Above the murmur came the soft, steady chant of a warrior. The light closest to Whiskey Jack started to spin around, growing large and larger with each revolution, until it formed into the misty figure of a warrior in full battle dress. The war paint on his face glowed in the darkness, and he held a sharp tomahawk in one hand and a spear in the other.

"I heard you wanted to fight us, Whiskey Jack," the warrior said. Behind him, the bobbing lights were growing taller and changing into the misty figures of many native men dressed for war. The phantoms nodded and murmured to themselves, drawing closer to the trembling Whiskey Jack.

Underneath the river pilot, the heartbeat in the ground was throbbing faster and faster, until bits of bark and twigs fell from the trees.

"With both hands tied behind your back," whispered another phantom warrior, right into Whiskey Jack's ear. The river pilot gave a yell of terror as he was yanked upright and his hands pulled behind his back and tied together. The phantoms gave a war shout, and the first warrior swooped toward Whiskey Jack, brandishing his tomahawk. Whiskey Jack gave a horrible scream and leapt off the mossy slope and ran down the incline toward the raft. The phantom's war-whoop had wakened the other raftsmen. They took one look at the ghosts and started casting off from the island, willy-nilly, waiting just long enough for Whiskey Jack to jump aboard before rowing with all their strength for the opposite shore. By the time they reached it, the island was once again dark and silent, and the crickets were chirping softly in the underbrush.

The crew untied their pilot without comment and floated the raft a mile or two downriver before Whiskey Jack gave the order to tie up again for the night. No one dared say anything to the massive pilot about the ghosts—not then, and not ever. But it was noted that from that day on, Whiskey Jack never stopped at the haunted island. And he never scoffed at another ghost story. He'd learned his lesson.

7

The Fishing Shanty

I'm telling you straight: folks these days don't seem near as colorful as the frontier folks I knew in the past. Seems like nowadays everyone's cut from the same cloth, don't you know. Yep, we don't have characters like Bluenose Brainerd anymore. Guess you needed a wild frontier to produce fellows like him.

Brainerd claimed to have arrived in Wisconsin via hot-air balloon. He hopped aboard in Nova Scotia and sailed here on a strong breeze. Well, that wind gave out over the north woods, and bang! He crashed right on top of a huge white pine tree. Brainerd was stuck up there eating bark and a few quail eggs and such until late fall when some lumberjacks cut down his tree and inadvertently rescued him.

Brainerd spent the rest of the fall and winter in the lumber camp showing those brawny men how they do things in Nova Scotia. Then he hightailed it to the nearest settlement and stole the town sweetheart right out from under the other blokes' noses, one, two, three. She was a high-spirited gal married to a high-spirited fellow, and boy, did the sparks fly between the two of 'em!

Brainerd built a fancy house smack dab between the river and the lake and then constructed a big barn for his cow and horses. They had a kitchen garden and some chickens and such, but they didn't clear any fields for wheat, since Brainerd wasn't much of a farmer. He made his money from trapping and hunting and some lumberjacking in the winter.

Oh, the tales they told in the settlement about the Brainerds! When the missus came to town one day to buy some dry goods, she asked Bluenose to water her geraniums. Brainerd didn't fancy the task. To show his missus who was boss, he tossed the flower pots into the river and then sat beside his fishing shanty reading last week's newspaper. When the missus came home, she found her geraniums piled up against a dead log at the bottom of the river, soaked clear through. She didn't say nothing to her husband then, but when he asked her the time a piece later, she chucked his watch into the river and told him: "If you want to know the time, Mr. Brainerd, go see for yourself!"

They were always trying to one-up each other. When Bluenose announced it was his turn to go to town, the missus insisted on going along. Brainerd fumed the whole time he was hitching the two-section front and back carriage to the horse, but then he got an idea that made him smile so wide that Mrs. Brainerd should have been suspicious. He assisted her quite graciously into the back section of the carriage, put himself in front, and drove to the top of the hill. Then he pulled out the pin holding the two parts of the carriage together and watched his wife roll backward down the hill. "There now, Mrs. Brainerd! I told you, you ain't going to town," he shouted down to his astonished wife.

When Brainerd forgot to open the flue to the stove and the smoke drove the couple out of the house, the missus took after

THE FISHING SHANTY

him with a pitchfork. When the missus bought a fancy new hat instead of the new leather she was supposed to buy Brainerd so he could make a harness, he tied the laundry in knots and hung it from the roof of the barn. When the missus sent Brainerd to get rid of a stray cat that was bothering her, he got himself so lost in the woods that he had to follow the cat to find his way home. When the cat drank up all the cream in the pantry the next morning, Mrs. Brainerd chased her husband around and around the barn, waving a rolling pin. And so it went.

Folks looked forward to church on Sunday, knowing there would be a new Brainerd story to share after service each week. The antics of that high-spirited couple were legendary!

One day, Bluenose came home from town with a very old accordion he'd bought off a lumberjack he'd met in the tavern. Bluenose was fond of music, and he carried the old accordion home under his arm, whistling cheerfully all the way. As soon as the chores were done, he settled into his favorite armchair by the window, leaned back against the cabin wall, and let her rip. Unfortunately, the accordion was more squeak and groan then melody, and Brainerd had a voice best compared to the moans of an injured cow. Mrs. Brainerd listened to about thirty seconds of the racket before tossing a pan full of dirty dishwater on his head and ordering him to get that "push-me pull-me organ" out of her house.

Brainerd knew better than to argue with his missus when she was in that mood. He'd seen her rout a bear once by setting fire to her petticoat and shoving it over the bear's head when it threatened to eat her chickens. It was best to beat a hasty retreat when she got that gimlet gleam in her eye. So he tucked the accordion under his arm and went out to his fishing shanty perched on the bank of the river. It was far enough away from the house that his singing wouldn't bother the missus, but close enough that he could get back in time to do the chores afore bed.

Bluenose sang a few bars of his favorite lumberjack song to warm up, and then he lit into that accordion like a wild bronco. He sawed away with one arm and hit random chords with the other, singing about Susannah and Polly Wolly Doodle and poor old Clementine. He made enough racket to wake the dead—and that is exactly what he did. The ghost of a drowned lumberjack who haunted the bank of the river came floating over to see what all the fuss was about. When he saw that accordion, he lit up like a firecracker, pulled up a log, and set down in the fishing shanty right across from Brainerd. Bluenose was surprised to see the ghost but recognized a fellow music lover as soon as the drowned man requested a round of Buffalo Gals.

Bluenose and the ghost sang so loud they shook the timbers of that fishing shanty, and the accordion squawked a merry accompaniment for them both. Finally, Bluenose said goodnight to the ghost and went to tend his stock before bedtime, but not before promising to return to the shanty on the following night for another hoedown.

When Bluenose arrived at the fishing shanty the next evening, he found that the ghost of the lumberjack had brought a friend. It was the ghost of an old hound dog that had drowned in nearly the same spot as the lumberjack. The spirit dog loved the sound of the accordion, and he howled along with the music while Brainerd and the lumberjack sang out of tune. It made an awful racket, and it attracted the attention of a couple of Indian braves who haunted the far shore. They came into the fishing shanty with their spirit drums to join the party. The fishing shanty was too small to fit them all, so Brainerd carried his accordion to the bank of the river, and they all sat down on a couple of fallen trees to make some music. What with the howling and the drumming and the squeaky accordion and the out-of-tune singing, the din they made reached all the way up to the house, where the missus was making a pie for dinner the next day.

Now, Mrs. Brainerd might have forgiven the ungodly racket if the men and dog hadn't been joined by the spirit of a strangled bride, who wrung her hands in despair and who screeched and wailed with a high soprano voice that pierced the eardrums and sent shivers down the arms and legs. The strangled bride was the last straw as far as Missus Brainerd was concerned. She let out an angry shriek that put the best efforts of the strangled bride to shame and came charging out of the house with a pitchfork in her hands.

"Mister Brainerd," roared the missus, her voice rising straight up the octaves until it reached a high C. "What is all this noise!"

Bluenose and the ghosts turned to look toward the house. Charging toward them like a steam train at full throttle came Mrs. Brainerd, brandishing her pitchfork. Her eyes were blazing like fire, and she had swelled up to the size of a large bull. The ghosts took one look at her and went running, floating, and galloping for the hills, according to their respective traditions. The strangled bride fainted dead away and was dragged from the scene by the drowned lumberjack.

Brainerd went running right along with the specters, but he was at a disadvantage, since he couldn't float over the river like the Indian warriors. He tossed the accordion to the other side and swam for dear life against the current while Mrs. Brainerd shrieked and scolded and waved her pitchfork at him.

Bluenose hid out on the opposite shore of the river for two days, playing sadly on his accordion. Finally, Brainerd decided that he'd had enough of music to last him a lifetime. He buried the accordion on the spot and walked home in the light of early morning to tell his wife he'd given up his music career for good, for which she was most thankful. But the ghost of the drowned lumberjack refused to leave the fishing shanty, hoping that one day Brainerd would dig up his accordion and they could have another rip-snorting hoedown.

Sometimes, when the moon was full, Brainerd and his missus would hear the ghost of the lumberjack singing sadly (and badly) in the old fishing shanty: "Buffalo gals, won't you come out tonight/And dance by the light of the moon." Then Brainerd would say: "It's too bad to disappoint the poor fellow." And Mrs. Brainerd would give her husband a look that promised him the sharp end of the pitchfork if he ever played the accordion again. And Brainerd—reminded of the way his missus had routed all the ghosts at the previous hoedown—would decide that discretion was truly the better part of valor and settle back into his chair to smoke his pipe instead.

8

In Midair

BARABOO

We've always been a circus family. My parents were aerialists, so I grew up wandering from pillar to post with a small-town circus in the south, learning to fly through the air high above the ring on the trapeze. I met my wife—a bareback rider—when my folks and I joined the Ringling Brothers Circus. As soon as my sons and daughter were old enough to "fly" with me, my parents retired to a small house in Baraboo near Ringlingville, the winter quarters of the circus.

It was a good life. Regular pay, enough travel to satisfy my wanderlust, and nice winter quarters in which to recoup and try out some new acts for the next circus season. My wife taught the kids their A-B-Cs and mathematics enough for them to get by as adults, and together we taught them everything we knew about the flying trapeze and stunt riding.

Molly, my youngest, took to horses as if she were part centaur. Her skills on the trapeze were adequate at best, but on top of a horse she could do things I've never seen before or since. She wanted to work with horses full-time, but we needed her in the act, and so her wish went unfulfilled until the Ringling Brothers bought the Forepaugh Sells Brothers Circus, and a pair of trapeze brothers with curly dark hair, twinkling gray eyes, and muscles of sheer steel joined the act.

Hank and Eddie had talent—nearly as much as my own sons, though I wouldn't say so to them. I was getting older now and was ready to hand over the fancy antics to the younger set while I created the routines and did some of the catching. Molly was written out of the act so she could do stunt riding full-time, and Eddie, the younger brother, took over her tricks while Hank relieved me of some of the more strenuous parts of the act.

That first season with the two new aerialists jazzing up our act and Molly performing stunts on horseback was one of the best I'd ever experienced, even though we had some hardships during the summer. A twister landed near the big top during one performance and carried it off, killing three folks and setting several of the wild beasts free. That was a night of pandemonium, let me tell you! In another town, the dam gave way one night after we went to bed and a wall of water washed right through the fields where we'd set up our circus village. My wife is a firm believer in omens, and she told me that things always go in threes. Something else was sure to happen, she said. Just wait and see.

We finished the season on a high note in spite of my wife's predictions and retired to Ringlingville for the winter. My folks were glad to see the grandkids and eager to help out with the act. Pa and I began writing a fancy new aerial routine for next season, while Ma and my wife repaired the costumes and helped Molly develop some new bareback riding tricks. Things were going along peacefully, with no sign of a third dire happening, when a registered letter arrived for Hank.

Hank was tickled pink when he read the contents of the letter. His maternal uncle Henry—for whom he had been named, but whom he had never met—had recently passed away, and the will named Hank as his heir. The amount he was to receive was astounding, and it meant that—if he wished—Hank would never have to work another day in his life. According to the will, if anything happened to Hank, the money would then pass to his brother Eddie, since Uncle Henry wished his fortune to remain in the family. Hank treated everyone in the act to dinner in a fancy restaurant that night, and we toasted to his good fortune. If Eddie was a little quiet during dinner, no one remarked on it.

Secretly, I was wondering if Hank would show up at the barn for rehearsal the next day. After all, he didn't need to work anymore. But he appeared right on time, though Eddie was a little late. My boys and the two brothers scampered up the ladders expertly, and soon they were flying overhead while Pa and I critiqued their style and technique.

High above our heads, Hank released the trapeze, performing a double somersault with a twist. He reached for Eddie, who was swinging toward him in preparation for the catch. Hank stretched out to his little brother, and missed his hands by a hair. Or did he miss? I could have sworn that both brothers were in perfect position to do the move. But somehow, Hank was plummeting toward the safety net, cursing his error. And then he was plunging straight through the safety net, which broke on contact, and into the hard floor, crushing his head and snapping his neck with a very final-sounding crack.

There was a split second of horrified silence, then yelling and screaming as we ran toward Hank, my sons and Eddie climbing down the ladders with a careless speed that would have earned them a scolding at any other time. It was immediately clear that there was nothing we could do for Hank, but we went through the formalities anyway, calling in the authorities and describing what had happened. In the end, the death was proclaimed an unfortunate accident caused by a fraying rope used to secure the safety net. We were admonished to keep our equipment in better order, and Hank was buried in the local cemetery.

I never said a word to anyone, but I knew that the "fraying rope" had been brand-new the week before the accident. I had strung it myself because the previous rope had looked a little worn. But after the accident, that new rope had strands hanging off it here and there, and the broken ends were so badly frayed it looked as if it were worn out. Something that could easily have been faked with a pocket knife. It looked to me as if the rope had been expertly cut to look frayed, with just a few strands left intact to keep the safety net in place. Any weight put upon the net would be enough to break the remaining strands, causing whoever fell on it to plunge right through to the floor.

Also, I found it very suspicious that Hank died so quickly after receiving the news that he'd inherited a fortune. Especially since I could have sworn that he did reach Eddie with room to spare. Sometimes in my dreams, I would see the brothers' hands meeting, and then Hank slipping out of Eddie's grasp. But in my dreams, Eddie deliberately pulled his hands away at the last moment, leaving Hank to fall on the damaged safety net.

But what could I prove? The deliberate damage to the rope could have been done by anyone, and there was no guaranteeing that Hank would be the first one to fall that day.

I was not the only one who harbored suspicions against Eddie. My family's manner toward Eddie became strained at best, and I could tell that my sons no longer trusted him; they changed the act just enough so that Eddie no longer had to catch any of the acrobats in midair. As soon as I realized this, I called a halt to practices until after the funeral. I was going to have to find a gracious way to move Eddie out of the act, but it was going to take some doing. To my relief, Eddie himself decided that the best thing for him to do was to retire from the circus and use his uncle's fortune to set himself up as a country gentleman. He made the announcement shortly after the funeral, and it lifted a weight off the shoulders of the whole family.

Eddie and I were the last ones to leave after rehearsal the day after the funeral—his last day with the act. After cleaning up and making all the routine safety checks, I locked the barn and walked with Eddie through the snowy evening toward home. Small snowflakes batted our hair and cheeks as we walked, not talking. Eddie was uneasy with the silence. He broke it first, saying: "Things just aren't the same without Hank around."

I nodded and pulled my coat closer as a chilly wind blew around us.

"I hope you can understand why I'm quitting the act," he ventured after another awkward silence in which the only sound was the crunching of our boots on the snowy path. "I just don't think I can put my heart into it, now that Hank's gone. I blame myself, of course. If I'd started my swing a little sooner, Hank would still be with us."

As he stated this, the wind gusted over us so fiercely that it nearly knocked us to the ground. I gasped suddenly in terror as a glowing ball of light appeared in the swirling snow directly in front

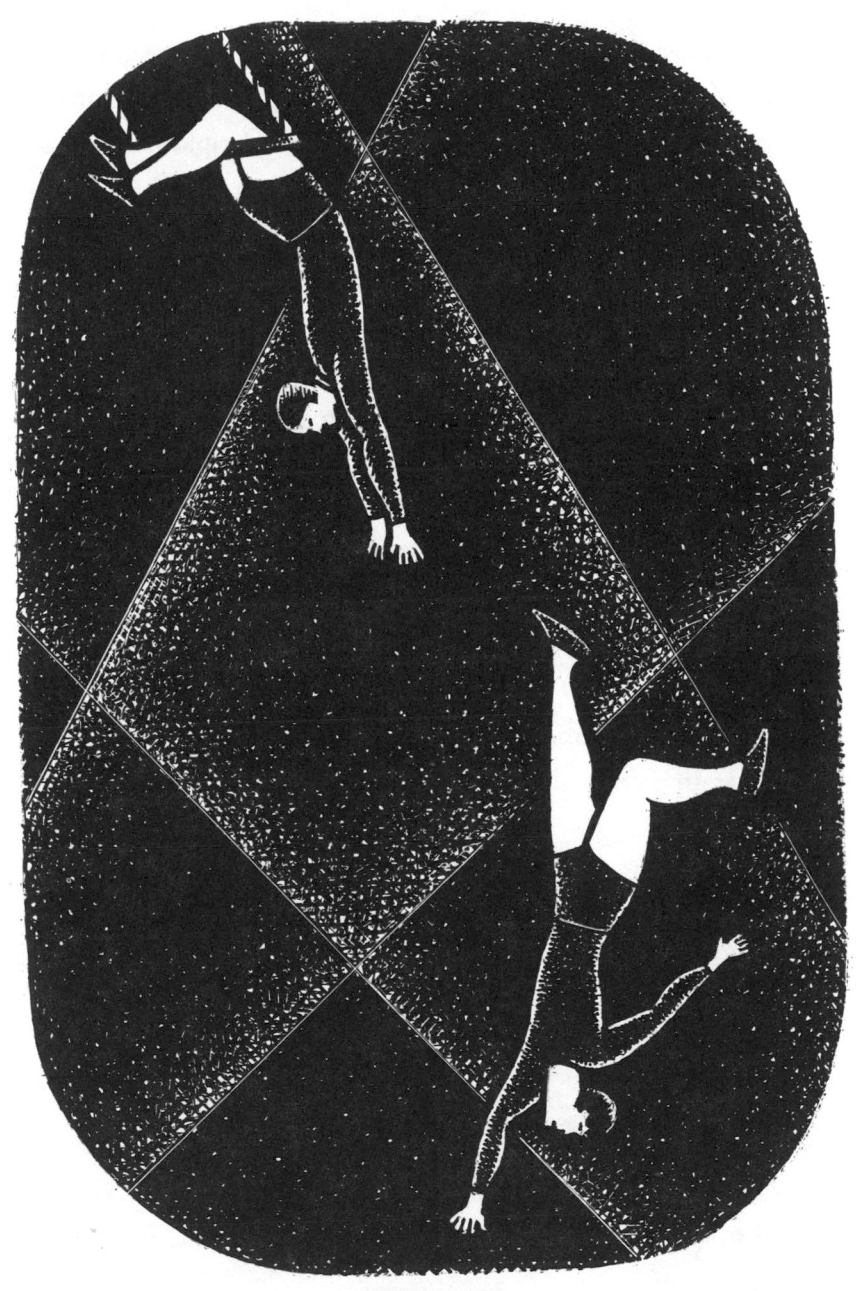

IN MIDAIR

of us. It transformed rapidly into the crushed figure of Hank, his bloody head lolling to one side on his broken neck. The phantom floated several feet above the ground, pulsing rapidly between white and blue in a manner that distressed the eyes.

"Eddie . . . " the spirit moaned, raising a costumed arm covered with sequins to point at his brother. "Eddie! Why did you drop me? Why did you kill me?"

Eddie gave a shriek of terror and cowered against me.

"I didn't kill you," he cried. "It was an accident. An accident!" His words ended in a guilty shriek.

"It wasn't an accident," Hank's specter moaned, growing larger and larger before our eyes. "You pulled your hands away. You let me fall."

"No, no! I didn't, I swear," cried Eddie, practically weeping in his terror.

"You cut the rope holding the safety net. You let me fall to my death. All for the sake of money, Eddie. My money. MY MONEY!"

The ghost howled the last two words and came swooping toward Eddie and me, his bloody head lolling grotesquely as it reached for his brother's neck.

Eddie screamed and stumbled backward, falling for a moment in a snowdrift. I cowered away from the phantom as its hands closed around Eddie's neck. Then Eddie broke away and ran for his life back down the path, disappearing on the far side of the barn with the ghost chasing him through the swirling snow, still shrieking the words "you killed me" over and over again.

I wanted to follow Eddie, but I was frozen to the spot, my legs trembling so hard that I could barely move. At that moment, my eldest boy came trotting down the path, looking for me since I was late to supper.

"Da! Da, what's wrong?" he exclaimed, grabbing me before I fell over in shock. I gasped out the story, clutching at my pounding heart. My boy listened grimly to my story, then he escorted me home and went off with his brother to look for Eddie. They found him face down in the river with a broken neck and a crushed head.

Quite sensibly, the boys did not go down themselves to investigate until after the proper authorities had been summoned. The police were not happy to be called out to a second circus death in a week, but it was obvious from the footprints in the snow that Eddie had slipped on the top of the bank in his panic and had fallen onto the rocks below, and that he had been alone when he died.

I didn't tell anyone outside of the family about the appearance of Hank's ghost just before Eddie's fatal accident. I felt it best to let the brothers rest in peace side by side in the local graveyard without stirring up any more spirits by spreading disreputable tales.

The whole family cobbled together an act before the new season, and it was a hit from the start. About midway through the summer, I interviewed a couple of fellows who worked the trapeze act in a small western circus. I liked their style and thought they'd make a fine addition to our act, but you can bet that I made sure that neither of them had any rich relatives before I hired them. I'd learned my lesson.

9

Shootin' the Ghost

It all started with the fire in our hay barn. It was a clear night—not a cloud in the sky or a rumble of thunder in the cold winter air—and yet suddenly the barn was on fire. I roused my family and we went running through the snowdrifts to see what we could do. The neighbors arrived shortly thereafter to help with a bucket brigade. In the end, we kept the fire away from the house, but the hay barn burned to the ground.

Lucky for us, we had a second barn on the property, though we were hard up for hay. Thankfully, it wasn't long until spring, and the animals made it through the last few weeks of winter just fine. Then came the next fire in June of the same year. We lost our second barn, and quite a number of our animals. It was a terrible blow, mentally and financially.

The rest of June was taken up buying more stock and rebuilding the barn. It was exhausting work, and the whole family was disheartened by our financial loss. So the last thing we needed was a ghost. But suddenly, there it was, haunting the upper stories of our house. We first heard it at dinner one night. It was just me and the wife and our three almost-grown kids. We were stolidly eating our way

SHOOTIN' THE GHOST

through a meal of creamed potatoes and ham when we heard footsteps overhead.

"What was that?" asked my wife, alarmed by the sound.

"Maybe it's a burglar," said Charlie, my eldest son.

"Maybe it's an arsonist, come to burn our house down!" exclaimed my daughter, her eyes like saucers.

I grabbed my rifle, and Charlie and I went upstairs together on tiptoe. By the time we reached the top, the sound of footsteps had ceased. We searched all the darkened rooms, but there was no one there. We went back downstairs to report the complete absence of anyone in the house besides ourselves. As we settled back into our chairs, the footsteps started again. Charlie and I gaped at one another, and then I grabbed the gun and raced upstairs again. Instantly, the sound of footsteps ceased, and again, we found no one on the premises.

We were baffled and frustrated by our failure to find the intruder, and no one slept well that night. The whole family turned the house upside down the next day, searching for a sign of our unexpected visitor, but we found nothing. Yet the minute we sat down to dinner that night, after the cows were milked and the horses fed and bedded down in their stalls, the footsteps began again, pacing back and forth overhead. I had my shotgun handy, and leapt up the stairs faster than a coyote after a rabbit, but the footsteps ceased as soon as I set foot on the second floor. I charged into my bedroom, sure that I'd find the intruder in there, but it was empty. My sons were on my heels with lanterns. We made a thorough search of the second floor and found nothing.

Every night, the footsteps rang out overhead during dinner. For about a week, I'd race upstairs as soon as I heard them, but after awhile I gave it up. There was never anything to see. Things stayed maddeningly quiet until I went back downstairs, whereupon the footsteps would begin again. Finally, we concluded that a ghost had moved into our house. My wife and kids were spooked at the thought of sharing their home with a ghost, but it never did anything but pace, so gradually we got used it and did our best to ignore the whole thing.

My daughter suggested that perhaps the ghost had been haunting the old cow barn and had moved into the house after the barn had burned to the ground in June. It was as good an explanation as any I'd thought up myself. Over dinner one night, the family speculated on who the ghost might have been in life. I suggested that it might have been a soldier killed in 1832, when Black Hawk, the leader of a band of Sauk and Fox Indians, fought against the U.S. Army and militia for possession of his homeland. Charlie suggested that it might be the ghost of a hunter or trapper who'd died mysteriously on what was now our property, back when Wisconsin was a territory filled with endless forest rather than wide-open fields. My wife favored the theory that it was the tormented soul of a Jesuit priest, made to pay for all the crimes committed against the native tribes in the name of religion.

It was not too long after that conversation took place that the gosh-darn ghost started playing with our broom. My wife kept it out in the summer kitchen, which could only be entered from outside the house, and one morning she couldn't find it anywhere. Everyone joined in the search, and the broom was finally located under Charlie's bed. We teased my wife about her forgetfulness, and she protested that she'd put the broom back in the summer kitchen after dinner the previous night. We didn't believe her at the time, and by the time the kids finished their teasing, she half-believed herself that she'd forgotten to put it away. Until the next morning, when she entered the summer kitchen and found the broom missing again. This time, it was located in the hayloft of the new barn.

That broom didn't stay put one day that whole summer. We found it in the cellar, in the horse stall, out in the corn field, under the bureau, up in the apple tree. My wife was furious, and took to shaking her fist up at the ceiling each night when she heard the footsteps overhead. "You leave my broom alone," she'd call up to the ghost. But it never listened to her.

Deciding that desperate times call for desperate measures, I chained the broom to the wall of the summer kitchen to appease my irritated spouse. Then I locked the door and pocketed the key. That should take care of the ghostly antics, I thought, pleased with myself. But the next morning, when I unlocked the door for my wife, I found the chain in pieces on the floor and the broom lying out on the back lawn.

Eventually, we grew resigned to the footsteps and the missing broom and decided we'd just have to live with them. Whoever the ghost was, we figured he was here to stay.

Then one day in early autumn, my neighbor and I took our shotguns and went hunting through the woods and fields near my farm. At dusk, we headed for home, and my wife invited our neighbor to eat supper with us. We were about halfway through supper when the footsteps began overhead. My neighbor sat bolt upright with his fork halfway to his lips. "Who in tarnation is that?" he asked, staring around the table. He did a quick head count, and then frowned. "Do you have someone visiting you? Why didn't they come down to dinner?"

My wife flushed, and I frowned, not sure what to say. The kids didn't have any inhibitions about it. Stumbling over one another, they gabbled out the tale of the ghost who had moved into the house after the barns burned down.

"You mean to tell me you've been living with a ghost all these months?" my neighbor asked me incredulously. "What have you done to get rid of it?"

I blinked in surprise. "What can I do? It's a ghost! I've never even seen it. We've only ever heard its footsteps overhead."

"Well, it's time we did something about that," my neighbor exclaimed, taking his shotgun from the gun rack.

"What are you going to do?" my wife asked, alarmed at the way he was brandishing the gun.

"I'm going to scare the ghost away," said my neighbor.

"You are not going to shoot a loaded gun in my house," said my wife firmly.

"It ain't loaded," said our neighbor. "I used up the last shot hunting today. I'm just going to use it to scare that gosh-darn ghost!"

So saying, he crept up the stairs on tiptoe, then leapt into the upper hallway with a terrible scream and pulled the trigger of the gun. With an ear-shattering boom, the "unloaded" gun fired, sending plaster and wallpaper showering all over the hall. I ran upstairs and found a great big hole in the wall and my neighbor looking foolish.

"Did you hear that?" Charlie exclaimed, as the family crowded into the upper hallway.

"We *all* heard that," said my wife sarcastically.

"Not the gunshot. The moan," said Charlie excitedly. "I think he shot the ghost!"

"Nonsense. You can't shoot a ghost," said my wife, frowning terribly as she surveyed the hole in the wall. Sheepishly, the neighbor twisted the gun behind his back as if to hide it and began apologizing profusely. After letting him grovel for a few minutes, my wife relented and forgave him the misdemeanor.

We all trooped back downstairs and continued our interrupted meal. I kept waiting for the footsteps to begin again over our heads, but the second floor was uncharacteristically silent. Suddenly, Charlie said: "Did you hear that?"

"What?" I asked, straining my ears. Then we all heard it. A pathetic whimpering sound was coming from the root cellar. Grabbing a lantern, Charlie went down to see what was making the noise. We all crowded around the trap door and stared into the cellar as Charlie climbed down the stairs. By the time his foot hit the second step, the whimpering had ceased. We watched as Charlie searched the small cellar from end to end, but there was no one there.

"Good lord! Do you think I really got him?" asked our neighbor.

"Maybe," I said skeptically.

But apparently my neighbor's scare tactics had done the trick. We never heard another ghostly footstep again, and my wife's broom remained ever after where she placed it the night before.

10

Frozen Dawn

It was like our honeymoon all over again. The kids were in college now, and both of them had decided to work during the summer months, which left me and the wife free to tool about the Great Lakes in our Bermuda-rigged sloop for the whole month of August. We were headed for the Apostle Islands— probably our favorite vacation spot in the entire world—and we made good time that trip. Pulled into dock at the marina in Washburn, brought out our camping gear and our sea kayaks, and prepared to roam any and all of the twenty-two islands that were part of the park.

Our aim that first day was for Long Island, a small gem off the southern tip of Madeline Island. Located on the northwest tip of the Chequamegon Point barrier spit, it was shaped like a half moon with sandy beaches on the shoreline and forest in the center. Home to two lighthouses and the remains of a third, Long Island was surrounded by shallow water that prevented cruise boats from coming too close. Anyone wishing to camp on the island made their way by water taxi or private boats. That was fine by us. We liked the privacy of the island and always camped there the first night we arrived in the Apostle Islands

National Lakeshore. It was a great spot for bird-watching, being one of the nesting grounds for the endangered piper plover.

We turned in early after a sunset stroll along the beach. I slept deeply and would have been content to sleep the whole day through, but my wife woke me just before dawn, wanting to kayak around the island as the sun rose and the world awakened. The light was still dim, and there was no sound anywhere—no birds, no wind whispering in the trees, no rustle of nocturnal animals hurrying to their homes. The hush was so complete that it felt eerie. Neither my wife nor I was inclined to talk as we silently launched the sea kayaks and began softly paddling around the island toward the La Pointe lighthouse. The lake itself was like glass, barely lapping at the strangely silent shore. To me, the soft splashing noise made by our paddles was a desecration in that waiting silence.

As we drew near the spot where the ruins of the 1858 lighthouse lay hidden by the trees, a cold chill swept through the air, ruffling the water around the kayaks and making me sneeze. My wetsuit did nothing to alleviate the terrible chill, and for a moment, I thought I saw snowflakes in the crystal-clear air around us. Then my wife gasped aloud and pointed. I tore my eyes from the snow and followed her gaze.

To our left was a wrecked barque laying in about seventeen feet of water with her bow pointing to the east. Her rigging stretched like skeletal hands up out of the depths, the only piece of her visible above the water. Lashed to the masts— one in the main and two in the mizzen—were the bodies of three dead sailors, covered with ice. One figure was heavily dressed, but his feet were bare and his heavy mustache was hard to discern beneath the ice that crusted it. Another had a

FROZEN DAWN

sandy beard and heavy clothes with high-topped boots. The third was just a small man, quite young, with light clothing unsuitable for the terrible cold and high-topped boots. The look on their frozen faces would haunt my dreams for many months to come.

"Dear God in Heaven," my wife whispered, her words producing a white cloud in the frigid air. We stared at the wreck in fear and awe as the grayness of dawn was slowly replaced by color. The first rays of the bright summer sun came over the horizon, piercing the grisly scene so that it shimmered and then faded away.

Warmth returned to the world with the disappearance of the ghostly vision, breaking the uncanny hush that had filled the predawn hour. Suddenly, the wind was dancing across the water of the lake, stirring and rippling it softly around the kayaks, and birds were singing and scolding and flapping around on the shore of the island.

"Were we dreaming?" my wife asked shakily, paddling back a foot or so in her nervousness. Wordless, I pointed to the front of my kayak, where ice was slowly melting away in the heat of the summer sun.

"There . . . there are snowflakes in your hair," my wife whispered. I reached up and touched one, and it melted on my fingers.

"I'm going back to the campsite," my wife said abruptly, expertly turning the kayak and hustling through the waters at top speed. I had a hard time keeping up with her.

We beached the kayaks and walked back to the tent together.

"Honey, what was that?" she whispered, huddling close to

me. I put my arm around her, as much to comfort myself as to comfort her.

"I think we caught a glimpse of the shipwreck of the *Lucerne*," I told her solemnly.

The *Lucerne* was a schooner barge that had grounded just off Long Island in a November gale in 1886. She arrived in Ashland in tow to the steamer *Raleigh*. The *Lucerne* was loaded up with 1,256 tons of iron ore consigned to Luttle, Ogleby & Co. of Cleveland. She set out to rejoin her tow steamer in Sault Sainte Marie, Ontario, but charged headfirst into a nor'easter instead. Caught in heavy snow squalls and gale-force winds, the *Lucerne* turned and tried to reach the safety of Chequamegon Bay. She was in view of the LaPointe lighthouse when she wrecked, and all of her crew was lost. Several men were swept overboard, and three of the sailors—those we had seen—had lashed themselves to the masts in attempt to save themselves from the frigid waters of Lake Superior. It hadn't worked.

Both the lighthouse keeper and early morning fishing boats discovered the wreck, and rescue boats arrived in the early afternoon to remove the bodies from the rigging and take them to Ashland for identification. The stern of the ship was found a half-mile east of the lighthouse with the words "*Lucerne*, Cleveland" painted on her arch board. The body of the mate washed ashore soon afterward, but the other crew members were never found.

My wife sat on the ground in front of our tent, hugging her knees with both arms as she listened to the tale of the wreck. "Those poor, poor men," she whispered, wiping a tear from her cheek. I nodded soberly, remembering their faces underneath the ice. We sat silently for a long time, listening to the awakening island and thinking our own thoughts. Then my wife rose to her feet and said: "I think I'd like to leave the island right now, Honey. I hope you understand."

And I did. I too wished to leave behind this haunted place. We packed up our belongings, stowed them in the kayaks, and paddled northward toward Madeline Island. Neither of us looked back.

We didn't report our strange adventure to anyone in the park. Who would believe it? Even now, I have a hard time reconciling myself to the memory. If my wife hadn't seen it too, I would have dismissed the whole thing as a dream. But we both saw it, plain as day, and the memory is etched inside me for all time. I'm not sure if I will ever return to Long Island again. Maybe. But if I do, I won't go kayaking at daybreak. I'll leave those predawn hours to the ghosts.

11

Barn Dance

As I drove down the seemingly endless dark road, I cursed myself for ever having listened to my friends. "It will be fun," they said. "A quaint little bar in the middle of nowhere," they said. "Great beer on tap. Gotta try it." Right. Sure.

About the only thing they'd gotten right, as far as I could make out, was that the location of the bar was the middle of nowhere. They'd hit that one bang on the nose. The bar was so far out in the middle of nowhere that I'd become completely and utterly lost trying to find it. I was pretty sure I would die of old age before I ever made my way out of this endless labyrinth of dark woods, dark fields, and ruined buildings. There was not one blessed sign of civilization anywhere to be seen.

Surely there must be a farmhouse somewhere on this benighted, twisty road where I could ask for directions back to Madison. Assuming I was still in Wisconsin, that is. I'd driven long enough by now to be in California. What a wretched, wretched night this had turned out to be.

It was at this juncture in my whining that the sound of music drifted through the open car window. I slowed down, listening. Then I caught a glimpse of a lighted building down a road that branched off from the one I was traveling. I turned at once, heading toward the lights and music. Civilization at last!

I slowed down after a moment when the road turned into a dirt lane. My headlights caught a number of wagons, carriages, buckboards and buggies parked beside a huge round barn. I whistled at the scene. Some rich folks had really gone to town for this party, I thought, parking near a fancy carriage with a horse hitched to the front. The bay horse blinked placidly at me as I got out of the car and headed for the lighted building.

The party was in full swing as I stepped through the large double doors. The building had obviously been converted long ago from a working barn to a dance hall. The center of the barn was filled with singing, swirling dancers in merry outfits that spanned every color of the rainbow. The dancers were all dressed in the costumes of yesteryear, reinforcing my impression that the people attending this party had gone to a great deal of trouble to recreate an authentic nineteenth-century barn dance.

I stood in the doorway admiring the huge, converted barn around me. The horse and cow stalls to my right had been replaced by a large alcove lined with tables full of good things to eat. The stalls to the left now contained benches filled with laughing, chatting folk, and a pot-belly stove had been installed near the door. Above our heads, the hay lofts remained in place but were filled with playing children and giggling teenagers sweethearting in the semidarkness. At the far end of the huge dance floor, a makeshift stage stood under the hayloft. An old-time band was sawing away at fiddle, guitar, jug, banjo, and so forth while a man with a shock of white hair and a large handlebar mustache called out the figures to the swirling dancers on the floor.

A large bearded chap clapped me on the shoulder in greeting and handed me a mug of beer. I took a sip and then gulped it down eagerly. It was the best beer I'd ever tasted. I was sure the quaint little nonexistent bar in the middle of nowhere had nothing to touch it. I'd landed on my feet, alright. My feeling of goodwill was enhanced when a dark-eyed beauty grabbed me by the hand and pulled me out onto the dance floor to make up a square with her and her friends. I hadn't square-danced since primary school, but it all came flooding back during that magical evening. I swung my partner and do-si-doed and even managed to do a star at the center with the other fellows. I was flying high, dancing and drinking, and singing along whenever the band played one of the old-time songs I'd learned as a little fellow at school. I forgot all about asking for directions and meeting my friends at the bar.

It wasn't until midnight, when the band took a break and I stood with my new acquaintances before a table lined with drinks, that I remembered to ask where I was.

"At the barn dance, silly," giggled my inebriated beauty. "Give us a toast to the night," she added, thrusting another beer at me. I cuddled her close to my side and raised my mug.

"To a delightful night," I said, loudly enough for everyone in the vicinity of the table to hear me. "And to a delightful party. Good fortune and long life to everyone present."

The crowd went silent when they heard my words. The stillness grew, flowing outward from me like a wave, until you could have heard a pin drop. As I glanced uneasily about me, wondering why my words had caused such a dramatic reaction, I saw the skin slowly peeling away from the merry faces, until all that remained were bone, rotting skin, and staring eye holes. A

BARN DANCE

few faces had the withered gray skin of a mummy, with maggots writhing grotesquely under cheek and chin. And the girl in my arms was nothing but a skeleton in a moldy blue dress. With a gasp of horror, I dropped my mug and leapt away from the skeleton. The mug hit the floor with a loud bang. It was completely empty now, although just moments earlier it had been foaming with beer.

There came a long sigh from the foul corpses in the barn. And then the lights went out. I screamed in terror and stumbled backward, slamming into a damp, foul-smelling pile of hay in the absolute darkness. Next I ran into a post and then got tangled up in some old rope as I frantically tried to find my way to the door without the use of my eyes. I kept expecting withered, bony hands to grab me, or the skeleton in the blue dress to reach out for a kiss. I couldn't see a thing as I slammed into the open door of a stall. It knocked the wind right out of me and made me pause long enough to realize that moonlight was streaming through a small hole in the ceiling. I used it to orient myself, spotting the barn doors a moment later. I rushed toward them, my feet crashing again and again through the rotten floorboards. In my panic I thought I'd never escape the old round barn. Then I was out in the moonlight and running to my car, which was parked beside a rotting wagon that had lost its wheels eons ago.

I leapt into the car and backed down the lane as fast as I could go, screeching my tires as I turned the car. My headlights caught the barn, which only had half of its roof and was sagging sadly to one side. Vines grew up and over the gloomy remains. Obviously, it hadn't been used in a very long time. I slammed the car into gear and drove as fast as I could away from the horrible, rotting barn with its dancing corpses.

Somehow, I found the highway and made my way, trembling, back to my home in Madison to spend the remainder of that restless night sleeping with the light on in my bedroom.

To this day, I have no idea where I was or how I managed to stumble across the ghostly barn dance in the middle of nowhere. Truthfully, I don't want to know. I heard later that folks in Vernon County sometimes hear strange music drifting over the hills at night, though no one can identify its source. And in my mind, I can see again the bright lights spilling out into the lane, and the bright happy faces of the ghostly farmers dancing the night away in a rotting old barn.

12

Firestorm

PESHTIGO

My teenaged grandson Jerry came bursting through the screen door into our big, old-fashioned kitchen, his dark hair awry and face as white as a ghost.

"Kiddo, what's wrong?" I asked immediately, abandoning the fishing fly I was carefully crafting at the huge oak table in the center of the room.

"Grandpa! You won't b . . . believe it!" Jerry stammered a bit in his intense agitation.

"Believe what?" I said, grasping his shoulder to steady him a bit. I guided him into one of the ornate handmade chairs that surrounded the large kitchen table.

He glanced sideways at me, suddenly shy and embarrassed. "Spit it out, kid," I snapped. "What won't I believe?"

"I think I saw a ghost," Jerry mumbled to the tabletop, unable to look me in the eye. "It was bright red, and it b . . . burned! I could tell it was a person, but the figure was a ball of flames, and I couldn't tell if it was a man or a woman."

"Where did you see the ghost?" I asked, keeping my voice calm and soothing. Jerry looked up from the table, surprised by my instant acceptance of the unbelievable.

"You believe me? That I saw a real ghost, I mean?" he asked.

"Of course I do," I said. "Was it over by the cemetery in back of the museum?"

Jerry nodded. "I was walking home past the cemetery, and I glanced inside and there it was." He paused and gulped suddenly, his gray eyes full of fear. "I stopped for a moment, trying to figure out what I was seeing. At first, it was just this bright red ball of light, like a gigantic firefly. But then . . . " he stopped and twisted his hands together in his lap, breathing heavily in agitation. "Then, whoosh! It turned into a tall figure engulfed in flames. My whole body jerked like lightning went through me, and I wanted to run, but my legs wouldn't move. I just stood there, watching it burn!"

Jerry paused again and looked back at the polished tabletop. He rubbed at a small smudge on the smooth wood, as if he could rub out the memory along with the dirt on the table. "The worst part . . . well, the worst part was you could tell the ghost was in agony. Its mouth was a black hole, as if it were screaming in terrible pain, though I couldn't hear a sound. I could feel burning heat coming off it, and I thought my own skin was going to burst into flame. Then it fell face down on the ground and vanished!" The boy shuddered in remembered terror and then sighed with relief, as if telling me about it had helped ease his mind. He looked up from the smudged tabletop and his gray eyes met mine. "What was it, Grandpa?"

I sighed sadly and replied: "One of the victims of the great Peshtigo Fire of 1871. Quite a number of the people killed in the fire are buried in the cemetery behind the fire museum."

Jerry looked puzzled. "I thought the fire museum had something to do with the fire department," he said.

I shook my head. It was an honest mistake. Our grandson lived with his folks in New Jersey, and he had never learned about Wisconsin's terrible fire in his private, East Coast school. None of his yearly visits had ever included a trip to the fire museum, since Jerry liked sports and outdoor recreation more than history. On previous visits, we had taken him hiking and swimming and fishing while he was in town, rather than touring the local museums. Leaning back in my chair, I proceeded to give him a brief history of the Great Peshtigo Fire.

There was a terrible drought here in Wisconsin in the year 1871. Everything had dried up, and I do mean everything. Even the cedar swamplands and the always-moist peat bogs were like tinder, and many of the trees—including the pines—had lost their leaves early. Fire was on everyone's mind, and people were taking extra care to avoid starting a forest fire. The rivers and creeks were so diminished that a major blaze could easily jump right across their banks with ease. But the summer and early fall passed without a major incident, though small fires were numerous. Passing trains would send up sparks and start a blaze. Hunters' campfires would smolder unnoticed even after they'd been doused with water; fires started to clear stumps and debris got out of hand and burned small areas of woods, though they never reached town.

The situation got so bad—what with underground fires smoldering deep in those peat beds in the dried-up swamps—that smoke was constantly in the air. In fact, it got so thick and extensive that ships far out on Lake Michigan were forced to use foghorns when they approached the shore, because they couldn't see anything through the heavy smoke. Perhaps the most vulnerable of all were people living in the isolated homesteads that dotted the thick forestlands.

The itinerant preachers had a heyday with the situation, claiming that the world was coming to an end and that this was the prelude to Armageddon. Unfortunately, many of the settlers believed them and resigned themselves to their fate rather than seeking refuge when the fires drew near.

On October 8, the situation came to a head. A great fire erupted almost simultaneously all around the Upper Great Lakes area, including Wisconsin, Michigan, and Illinois. It was as if all those smoldering small fires converged simultaneously into one great blaze. Some folks think it was a windstorm that caused the terrible conflagration. Others think it was an unusually intense meteor shower—invisible through the heavy smoke cover—that rained down upon the dry land and started the blaze in multiple sites all at once. Whatever the explanation, suddenly forests, glades, villages, and towns were all ablaze.

The fire raged over twenty-four thousand square miles, primarily in Wisconsin and upper Michigan. On the same night, smaller forest fires also ravaged vast areas of lower Michigan, and to the south, the great city of Chicago. Whole families were burned to death in their homes. People racing to safety were overtaken as the fire spread with inconceivable rapidity and caught them, burning them to death as they ran. Fire whirls twisted off treetops. Flames would rise fifty feet from the top of the trees and leap over thirty acres of clearing to ignite the forests beyond. Marsh gases hovered above the ground like black balloons and then would explode, throwing fire in every direction. The whole country was lit by a fierce lurid glare. The direction of the wind changed rapidly, blowing first from the southwest, then from the west, then from the northwest, then back again from the south, causing a series of whirlwinds that showered cinders and sparks in every conceivable direction.

Here in Peshtigo, the first hint of the holocaust came on the wind, as light puffs of air began drifting across the town. Light slowly began to illuminate the horizon to the south, and the earth started to tremble. The village folk heard a distant roar coming their way. Even then, no one realized how great the danger was until the lurid glare of the fire lit the horizon from end to end, and the howling, spitting, shrieking fire rent the air, sounding like nothing but agonized cries from the depths of the infernal pit.

Then a tornado made of wind and fire hit the town, blowing down chimneys, ripping the roofs off houses, tossing a thousand-pound wagon end over end like a tumbleweed, and enveloping the town in tremendous sheets of flame. The firestorm fed on itself, creating internal winds of up to eighty miles an hour as it drew in oxygen and fuel. Panic-stricken, the settlers found themselves surrounded by fire with no apparent escape. People fled amid a barrage of falling embers and hot ash, their clothes and hair on fire. Families seeking shelter down in their cellars were asphyxiated. Others sheltering in wells and marshes were boiled alive.

Men, women, and children raced toward the bridge, hoping to escape the inferno that burned around them, but the bridge itself was already in flames. Hundreds crammed into the river, shoving sheltering cattle and other animals aside in their panic.

FIRESTORM

Many slipped under the water in the confusion and were drowned. Others were injured or killed as debris from the fire flew over their heads. Those in the water could only hold their heads above the surface for a few seconds at a time because of the intense heat, which caused floating debris to catch fire.

In less than an hour from the time the firestorm struck, the village of Peshtigo was completely annihilated. More than a hundred people perished either in the flames or in the water, and all property was wiped out of existence. The wooden ware factory, the water sawmill, the gristmill, the machine shop, and the sash factory, store, and warehouses—all gone. Houses, churches, schools, and other dwellings were completely destroyed. Charred and blackened embers met the eye no matter which way you turned, and the streets were littered with the frightfully mutilated corpses of men, women, children, horses, oxen, cows, dogs, swine, and fowl. Some people were so completely consumed by the fire that their remains could fit into the palm of a hand.

In the end, the vaporizing heat of the firestorm, which reached more than two thousand degrees Fahrenheit, began sucking cooler air from Canada and the western United States. This created counterwinds that grew strong enough to flow the fire back onto itself. Having no more fresh fuel, the great fire finally died out.

The Great Peshtigo Fire ended hundreds of human lives and completely destroyed an ecosystem. It took decades for the land to recover, and no family in the region was untouched by the tragedy. The true death toll would never be known, but it is estimated that more than one thousand five hundred people lost their lives in the flames.

When I finished my story, Jerry whistled softly through his teeth. "Horrible," he said. "No wonder I saw a burning ghost. There must be a lot of victims who can't rest in peace after such a blaze."

"I imagine there are," I replied, remembering the red balls of light I frequently saw bobbing in the backyard at dusk. Sometimes, at the sight of them, I would be overwhelmed by feelings of terror, pain, and despair; all the feelings that must have swept through the settlers of Peshtigo that fateful night so long ago.

I shook my head a little to clear away the memory, and said: "I'll take you to the museum tomorrow, if you'd like, so you can learn a little bit more about the fire."

"I'd like that. Thanks, Grandpa," Jerry said.

Deciding that we'd both had enough drama for one day, I shooed him off to the living room to watch TV while I went back to my fly making. Tomorrow would be soon enough for my grandson to learn more about the fire that claimed so many lives in its fury. For today, we would let the Peshtigo ghosts rest in peace.

PART TWO
Powers of Darkness and Light

13

The Dream

Sarah had been a bride for less than a month when her new husband took sick from the cholera. The epidemic swept through their small community that summer, killing many of the small children. She had never envisioned that the disease could touch her tall, strong husband—until the day when he came in early from the fields, pale and shaking with pain.

He had a bad case from the beginning; he could keep nothing in his stomach, not even water, and his leg cramps were severe. Sarah summoned the doctor at once, but he didn't hold out much hope. The rapid loss of so much of her husband's body fluids led to dehydration and shock. Within three days, her new husband was gone.

Numb with grief, Sarah went through the motions of choosing a coffin and arranging the funeral. It was only when they put the casket into the ground that the first terrible grief broke through the numbness. With a scream of agony, she tried to throw herself into the hole after it. It took the combined strength of both her parents to hold her back. They led their sobbing daughter back to her old home, which was next to the cemetery, and the doctor gave her a sedative. Sarah spent the long hours of the afternoon staring out the window toward the new grave and weeping. "At least he won't be too far from me," she told her Mama.

That night, after Sarah had cried herself to sleep, she had a very vivid dream. In it, she saw her husband, white and still, lying in his coffin underground. As she watched him, she saw him move! He started wiggling around as if he were trying to get comfortable in bed. Finally, he settled onto his left side—which he had always favored—and went back to sleep. Sarah woke with a panicked scream that brought her parents racing into the bedroom, nightclothes awry.

"He's alive. He's alive," Sarah cried, wringing her hands. "I just saw him moving inside his coffin!"

Thinking she'd had a nightmare, her father shook his head sadly and told Sarah that it was only a dream caused by her grief. Digging up the body would only prolong the agony she felt. Weeping softly, Sarah finally agreed to lie down again and sleep, though she was still convinced that her husband had been buried alive in the cemetery.

The next day dragged past for the whole family. Everyone was exhausted and weepy, and the bereaved widow kept staring over toward the cemetery, thinking about her dream. Or was it only a dream?

Sarah woke again, screaming, in the middle of the second night. Once again, the new widow had seen her husband in his coffin. He'd flipped over onto his right side, curled his legs up beside his stomach, and was using his arm as a pillow. "He's alive!" she told her parents hysterically. "We buried him alive!"

Her father realized then that he would have to dig up the coffin to prove to his daughter that her husband was truly dead.

THE DREAM

Nothing else would appease her. If he didn't do it, Sarah would go out there and dig it up herself with her bare hands.

So the father sent his wife to summon their next-door neighbor. Together, the two men dug up the new grave in the cemetery while the poor little bride watched with huge eyes and shaking body. Around one o'clock, they pulled the coffin out of the ground. The neighbor held up the lantern as the father pried off the lid. Everyone leaned forward as the lid was pushed aside, and then all gasped in shock. Just as Sarah had seen in her dream, her husband lay on his right side with his legs curled up next to his stomach and his arm supporting his head like a pillow.

"He's alive! I told you he was alive," Sarah gasped, tears streaming down her cheeks. She leapt forward and began shaking her husband by the shoulder.

"Wake up, love. Wake up," she begged him.

Her father pushed her gently aside and lay his head against the corpse's chest. "I hear a heartbeat," he said suddenly and began massaging his son-in-law's arms, chest, and face in an attempt to revive him. His wife and daughter clung together, and the neighbor held the lantern high as he worked over the young man.

Suddenly, the man's eyes fluttered open. "Brandy! Get some brandy," gasped the father. Sarah ran into the house and came back with a flask. Gently, the father poured a little brandy down his son-in-law's throat. He swallowed convulsively, choked, and then tried to sit up. With a cry of joy, Sarah threw herself against him, nearly falling into the coffin herself.

Gently untangling Sarah from her husband, the men lifted him out of the coffin and carried him into the house. The son-in-law was placed into a chair by the hot fire with heated salt bags under his arms and legs to warm him. By the next morning, he was back to normal, though he remembered nothing of his own "death" and burial.

Sarah and her husband lived happily together for another sixty years after his false death. They raised a family of eight children, who never tired of hearing about the dream that saved the life of their father after he had been buried alive in the local cemetery. Whenever he told the story, Sarah's husband would pull his wife into his arms and give her a hearty kiss full of love and gratitude, while the children hugged them both as tight as they could.

14

The Knocker

MINERAL POINT

I gave my tool kit a once-over, made sure my twelve freshly dipped candles were secure, and then put one foot into the small bucket and grabbed hold of the rope in the chilly dark gray light of predawn.

"Right, boys. Lower away," I said cheerfully to Robert and Pete, who were manning the windlass that morning. I swung out over the dense black hole that was the vertical shaft of the mine, and they lowered me into its depths. Thirty feet, then forty feet down I sank with one foot dangling over nothing and my tool kit firmly gripped in one hand. At fifty feet my free foot and the bucket hit the floor at the same moment. I stepped out into pitch black and gave the rope a couple of tugs to let the boys know I was down.

Somewhere far off down one shaft, my keen eyes caught the faint glimmer of candlelight that told me some of the other Cornishmen had already arrived at the diggings. I was an expert at darkness by now, and my talented fingers found and lit a candle without my brain having to engage in the exercise. We used only one candle at a time in this dark place, since it cost too much money to use more. I made twelve candles each morning to take with me for the day, saving all the wax drippings I could to bring home to help save money.

I stomped happily with my candle through the permanent dusk that was my underground world; through four-foot tall shafts where I had to keep my too-tall five-foot-five frame stooped; through tunnels where an underground spring kept the floor permanently soaking wet with a stream running down one side; through a couple of crawl spaces where the light of my candle was on one side while the bulk of my body was on the other as I squeezed myself through; and thus on to the promising vein of lead my mate Todd and I had discovered yesterday.

If the vein's rich, we'll 'ave to widen that narrow bit, I said cheerfully to myself. Todd had helped me drill the hole for the blast, and I was expecting him to show up soon to help me sort through the rubble for lead.

I examined the site carefully for instability—didn't want the ceiling coming down on our heads. All was well, and the stack of beams I had carried in with me would be needed only in a few strategic places. I shored everything up, taking extra precautions because you never can tell what a blast of dynamite might do to the ceiling and walls of a mine, up where you can't see.

When the spot was as secure as I knew how to make it, I began a careful exploration of the gray lumps of lead my sharp eyes had spotted in the light brown limestone. I worked slowly, taking great care to make sure all was stable before I moved deeper into the space created by the blast we'd set before leaving last night. I could hear the muffled sounds of voices and digging coming from other parts of the mine, and it comforted me to know I was not alone in the dark. Todd was late this morning, I thought, wondering if everything was alright at his house.

My candle started to flicker wildly up on the tiny opening where I'd wedged it. It was right down to the stub, so I returned to where my tools, candles, and lunch were stashed to get the second candle of the day. All the candles were gone! I gasped aloud in shock. I had encountered a few other miners on my way to the new diggings, but no one had come near enough to take my candles, and I hadn't dropped any. How could they have disappeared?

I heard a happy sniggering sound from the darkness behind me. The sly laugh bounced around and around in the flickering darkness that was barely penetrated by my single small candle, freezing my limbs and raising the small hairs on my arms and legs. I knew that sound. It was the laugh of a Knocker.

As if in response to my thought, I heard a soft rap-rap sound to my right. I raised the stub of candle and saw two of my other candles in a niche created by yesterday's blast. I stood on tiptoe and grabbed hold of them, lighting a new one before the one in my hand burned my fingers. I carefully put the third candle back in my toolbox, knowing that I'd need it to find my way out if I couldn't figure out where the Knocker hid the others or Todd didn't arrive soon with his daily supply.

Stumbling over the rock and gravel created by the blast, I searched for my candles. I'd found all but two by the time Todd came slipping through the tight space into the blast location. The Knocker sniggered several times while I searched, its shadow darting hither and thither in the candlelight. Now and then it rapped lightly on the stone above my head.

The Knocker greeted Todd with a shower of small pebbles. "'Ey," Todd protested, ducking his head and trying to shield his candle with the boards he'd brought to help prop up the blast site. "T'aint the ceiling stable, Jack?"

"She's stable. 'Tis only the Knocker, trying to bother thee," I replied absently, my eyes spotting the final two candles underneath a largish rock full of lead. I pulled them out and stuck them into my pocket.

"The Knocker?" asked Todd in astonishment, putting down the boards he was carrying and beginning a careful inspection of the supports I'd constructed for walls and ceiling. The Knocker sniggered in the shadows, and Todd paused in his inspection, his dark eyes growing wide with surprise. "I thought we left that lot back in Cornwall," he said, fumbling in the pocket where he always kept one of the Cornish pasties his wife baked for his lunch. He pulled it out, nipped off a large piece, and set it carefully on the ledge where I'd propped my candle. *Now why hadn't I thought of that?* I wondered.

"There's enough lead 'ere to fill a car. I'm going to h'ask the boys to lay some track this way," I said to Todd. "See if thee can widen that narrow bit while I'm gone."

"Right-o," he replied as I lit another candle to take with me. As I slipped through the narrow place, I glanced back to the ledge holding the candle. The piece of pasty was gone.

The Knocker was quiet the rest of the day, except for a few showers of pebbles and some rap-rap-rapping on the walls of the mine. Guess the pasty appeased its teasing spirit.

As I made my way down the Merry Christmas Mine hill toward the small row of stone cottages where I lived with the missus, I thought about the Tommyknockers. My grandpappy told me that they were the spirits of departed miners. When visible, they took the form of little old men with small bodies and big ugly heads with too-large ears and noses. They wore peaked hats, leather jackets, and water-soaked leather boots.

Happy Tommyknockers helped miners find ore and rapped on the walls of the mines right before a cave-in. My old grandpappy told me to count the raps. More than three raps signaled a cave-in coming. Tommyknockers have saved the life of many a miner with their timely warnings.

Unhappy Tommyknockers—those who are ignored or cursed at—stole hats and tools, threw rocks, blew out candles, and tampered with dynamite fuses. We surely did not want an unhappy Knocker in our mine, I thought.

I told my missus and our little daughter all about the Knocker over supper, and then I stayed up carving and painting the rough image of a Knocker for several hours before the fire. For some reason, I gave him the face and clothes of my grandpappy, he who first told me about Tommyknockers. The next morning, I put my carving and an extra pasty baked by the missus next to my newly dipped candles and rode the windlass down into the mine.

Todd was already filling another car full of lead rock when I arrived. He nodded in satisfaction when he saw the carefully carved image of a Knocker that I placed up by his candle, along with the extra pasty. He patted his pocket and said: "M'wife also gave me an extra pasty for the little fellow."

"That should keep 'im 'appy," I said, setting down my pack. The Knocker rapped his agreement.

Things went very well with us for the next month. The Knocker brought us good luck. We'd found a large vein of lead, and our blasts went off without a hitch. Oh, sometimes the rascal would hide our tools in strange and sometimes amusing

THE KNOCKER

places and snigger at us while we searched for them, but it was friendly tomfoolery. He didn't bother the other miners too much, but concentrated his efforts on me and Todd.

News of the Knocker spread quickly through the whole mine. Soon, most of the men were bringing cakes, biscuits, and pieces of pasty to put beside the small carving I'd made.

One morning, I got news that Todd's father-in-law had passed away suddenly in the night and that Todd was not coming to work. So I made my way alone to the back of the large shaft we were digging along the vein of lead and left the usual offering of pasty next to the carving before starting the day's work. We'd intended to set another blast today, but it took both of us to work the drill and hammer, so I'd have to wait until tomorrow or ask one of the other lads to give me a hand. I decided to wait and turned my attention to carving out the last of the reachable lead.

The Knocker was very much in evidence that day. He blew out my candle twice, hid my pickaxe at the far end of the passage, and started rapping almost constantly on the walls: Rap-rap-tap-tap-rap. Rap-rap-tap-tap-rap.

"What's the matter, fella?" I asked in irritation as a hail of tiny pebbled pelted me from above.

I was answered by a heavy rap-rap-tap-tap-rap and more pebbles. Something about that last pebble shower made me uneasy. I glanced at the candle, which was trembling visibly as if in response to some massive, unseen force. Rap-rap-tap-tap-rap. The noise came again, louder than I had ever heard it before. Then the Knocker spoke. "Jack Trelawney, GET OUT!" it shouted, almost in my ear. The voice it used was that of my long-dead grandpappy.

I gasped, stumbled backward, and then fled up the shaft, accompanied by a rap-rap-rapping noise that turned into the thunder of a cave-in. Huge stones pelted my back and legs as I raced toward safety in the sudden darkness caused by the extinguishing of the candle. I tripped over the slippery, uneven floor and fell into a puddle, knocking my head so hard I saw stars in the blackness. I tensed, waiting for the ceiling to come down on my head, but all I could hear was the steady rumbling of the rocks settling at the far end of the passageway. I could feel blood trickling down my forehead, and there was a throbbing pain from a cut in my leg. But I was alive, and that was all that counted.

A light appeared suddenly, green-white rather than the warm yellow glow of the candle. It came from a little old man wearing a peaked hat, leather jacket, water-soaked leather boots, and the face of my departed grandpappy. He glared fiercely at me. "Jack Trelawney, thee little sod," said the Knocker, who was also the ghost of my grandpappy. "What did I tell thee about listenin' to Tommyknockers? Thee almost got thyself killed back there! Next time, pay h'attention when I rap more'n three times."

With that, the Knocker disappeared with a little popping noise, leaving me alone in the dark. But not for long. I could hear shouting and running feet as the other miners came hurrying toward my shaft to see if I had survived the cave-in.

I was bandaged up and sent home to recuperate while the men cleaned the mess, shored up the unstable shaft, and retrieved my tools. They even found the carving of the Knocker for me. Everyone marveled at how I'd managed to avoid what seemed like certain death, and I was quick to tell them of the Knocker who had rapped me a warning signal. I only told my missus and Todd the whole story—including the identity of the Knocker and the ferocious scolding I'd gotten.

"Serves thee right," said my missus, hugging me tightly with tears in her eyes. "Next time, listen when your grandpappy raps at thee!"

And Todd agreed.

15

Wolf Pack

It was a hard winter, deep in the woods of the new territory. Blizzard after blizzard left the settlers isolated in their small cabins. As food grew scare, the wolf packs came close, harassing anyone foolish enough to travel the icy roads to town. The men and boys carried rifles with them wherever they went, and more than one wolf was shot in the short distance between homestead and barn.

The Schultz family lived in a cabin more than seven miles from town, and their nearest neighbors—the Hanson family— lived over a mile away down a rough track through the woods. In winter, they were completely isolated, which had never bothered the Schultz family much until this hard winter when the wolves surrounded their house each night, howling and prowling the fence line until morning.

The young father, Mark Schultz, had two guns on the farm, which he kept loaded at all times. His son, James, was too small to handle the heavy gun with ease, so he made sure his wife, Maggie, and Jenna, his eldest daughter, knew how to load the gun and shoot straight. Maggie killed several wolves during the early part of winter when her husband was out checking his increasingly empty traps.

By the beginning of the new year, the wolves were hungry enough to hunt in daylight, and it became too dangerous for the husband to leave the little farm between blizzards. Food was tight, but they had enough to last the winter if they were careful.

The wolves were coming close to the house now. They would occasionally fling themselves at the door and windows after dark, trying to get at the family sitting snug inside the cabin walls. Little Minnie, the youngest Schultz, would shriek with terror when this happened and hide under her bed up in the loft, while Samson, the Schultz's dog, would growl and bark in outrage at the creatures menacing his family. Mark Schultz feared that the wolves might break the heavy glass panes of the windows, so he spent two days fashioning heavy shutters to cover them at night, and he added sturdy bars to reinforce the door of the cabin.

One morning in February, he came in from the barn to report that there were signs of digging around the edges of the barn door. The wolves were trying to get inside to eat the livestock. He spent the rest of the day fixing the barn doors and checking to make sure all the walls were secure. He shot at a wolf as he crossed the yard at dusk on his way in to supper, but the bullet only winged the creature, and it sprang away into the dark woods outside the fence line.

As Mark entered the cabin, his eldest girl opened the stove and threw in another log. The fire popped and sparked as the log hit the embers, and a few coals flew out the door. Father and daughter raced to find them all and stamp out the sparks.

"Careful there, Jenna," Mark said, patting her on the shoulder.

"Yes, Pa," Jenna said.

WOLF PACK

Unnoticed by all was a small coal that sat smoldering in a corner of the cabin behind the stove. As the family sat down to supper in the front room, the floor and wall of the kitchen slowly began to burn. The curtains caught fire, and the fire crept into the store of kerosene, which exploded.

The sound of the explosion brought the family to their feet with cries of alarm. Mr. Schultz made the mistake of opening the kitchen door to see what was wrong, and the fire surged into the front room.

"Get the children out to the barn, now!" Mark Schultz screamed to his wife as he beat at his hair to put out the flames. "Take the gun!"

Maggie grabbed one of the guns from over the door, removed the bar, and hustled her children toward the barn through the gathering dusk. Samson went flying past them with a growl and threw himself onto a wolf that had just leapt the fence into the yard. Three more wolves closed in on the dog, and Maggie was afraid to shoot for fear of killing the family pet. Keeping a tight grip on little Minnie's hand, she raced the children away from the burning house and into the barn, praying that the sparks would not ignite it as well.

She heard a shot a moment later, then Mark came leaping into the barn and slammed the door shut behind him.

"Where's Samson?" cried Jenna and James together. Mark didn't answer, and the family realized that the dog must have been killed by the wolves.

"I couldn't put out the fire," Mark said grimly to his wife. "We've got to hitch up the sleigh and drive out of here at once. If the roof catches on fire then the sparks will surely ignite the barn."

Maggie nodded. "Do we have any powder left for the guns?" she asked. Mark shook his head. The ammunition stored in the kitchen was gone. They had only one bullet left in the gun Maggie held.

They could no longer hear the wolves, who had been scared away by the burning cabin. This was the best chance they had to leave the farm safely. Maggie had loaded the children, the hens, and the small heifer calf inside the sleigh by the time Mark got the horses hitched up. Just in time too, for a section of the barn roof was already ablaze. They would have to leave the cow behind, since she could not keep up with the horses, which must outrun the wolf pack to save the lives of the family. Mark pushed the cow out the back door of the barn to fend as best she could in the snow. Little Minnie started crying when she realized they were leaving the cow behind, but there was nothing else they could do.

Sparks were flying everywhere as Mark drove out of the barn into the yard. Maggie looked behind once and saw the roof of the cabin collapse. The side of the barn nearest the house was already consumed with flames. They had left just in time. Now if they could make it to the neighbor's farm before the wolf pack returned . . .

As if on cue, the family heard howling coming from both sides of the road. Mark whipped up the horses and the heavily loaded sleigh slipped and slid down the snow-covered track toward the neighbor's farm. The horses screamed in panic as the wolves emerged from the trees, loping easily beside the sleigh. Six of them attacked the horses, nipping at legs and heads and flanks until blood streamed down their bodies. Several wolves flung themselves at the sleigh. Jenna and James beat at them with pieces of timber they'd brought from the barn, and Maggie slammed one after the other with the butt of the rifle, grimly saving the final shot until it was absolutely necessary.

Fear sped the horses onward in spite of their injuries. Behind them, the fire was leaping so high it lit the dark night, making the trees appear as dark silhouettes. A wolf sprang at them from the side of the road and landed on the seat beside Mark.

"Get away from Pa," Minnie screamed, leaping suddenly from her place between Maggie and Jenna. She beat at the wolf with tiny hands, overbalanced as the sleigh hit a bump in the snowy track, and fell out of the sleigh.

"Minnie!" Maggie screamed as the little girl tumbled into the snow. At once, the wolves pursing the sleigh whirled away and leapt upon the little figure. Minnie gave one terrified shriek and was silent as the wolves growled and snapped and fought with each other her tiny figure.

"Stop the sleigh," Maggie shouted to her husband as she fired their last bullet into the midst of the ravaging pack. Mark pulled hard on the reins, but the terrified horses barely slowed. As Maggie leapt to the edge of the sleigh, shouting her daughter's name, several of the wolves abandoned the poor, broken body and started chasing the sleigh once more. Maggie grabbed hold of the reins, trying to help her husband stop the horses so they could go back for Minnie, but at that moment a wolf flung itself into the sleigh, right on top of little James. Fear for her remaining children made Maggie turn. With a roar of sheer rage, she grabbed the animal by the scruff of its neck and hurtled it out of the sleigh in one movement.

"We've got to get the children out of here," Mark shouted. "There's nothing we can do for Minnie now."

Maggie nodded grimly, slapping another wolf away from the sleigh with the butt of her rifle.

By this time, the Hanson family had seen the fire and was on its way to help. The Hanson sleigh suddenly appeared on the narrow track, and shots rang out as their neighbors tried to drive the wolves away from the fleeing Schultz family. Mr. Hansen swerved his vehicle aside to let the runaway Schultz sleigh through while his sons reloaded the rifles. Then they shot again and again into the pack until the wolves gave up the chase.

The Schultz sleigh thundered into the neighbor's yard, the horses halting abruptly when the road ended in a huge pile of wood. Mrs. Hanson and her daughter came running outside. They each took one of the weeping Schultz children and brought them inside. Mark and Maggie staggered in at their heels, and Mark begged Mrs. Hanson for ammunition so that he could go back down the road and retrieve their youngest child from the wolves. While Mark was reloading his rifle, Mr. Hanson came gravely into the house. In his arms he carried a tiny, ravaged bundle of blood and cloth.

Maggie gave a moan at the sight and fainted. With a sigh of agony, Mark took the savaged remains of his youngest daughter into his arms and wept.

Bereft of all their belongings as well as their youngest child, the Schultz family stayed with the Hansons until the spring. Then they sold their horses and used the money to go back to Mark's family in Ohio, never to return to the wild frontier.

They say that sometimes, on winter nights, people passing that way can still hear the ghostly howl of the wolf pack and a frantic mother's screams as she tries in vain to save her youngest child.

16

Helene and the Loup Garou

Etienne spent much of his early life roaming the Great Lakes as a *voyageur*—an explorer, that is—and a fur trader, following in the footsteps of the "black robes," the name by which the Jesuit priests were known among the native tribesmen. He was thirty-five when he met Isabel at a settlement in Quebec and toppled into love for the first time. After a whirlwind courtship, the two married, and Etienne tried to settle down by taking a job in town. But he was an explorer at heart, and a few years after his daughter Helene was born, he once again began traveling the Great Lakes, exploring and trading furs.

Isabel—still crazy about her man even after a decade of marriage—finally put her foot down. If he was going to travel, they would travel together as a family. And that was that. From that day on, the family traveled hither and yon, and little Helene was raised on the road. They would settled at various outposts along the Great Lakes for a year, maybe two, and then her parents would move on to the next rich source of beaver.

When Isabel reached the town of La Baye on the western shores of Michigan, she fell in love with the wild beauty all around her. This, she told Etienne, was where they would build their permanent home. It was the perfect place—right on the bay. If the settlement had more English folk than French, what of it? Here in the wilds of the west, survival was more important than ethnicity.

Helene was ten when they settled in La Baye, and for the first time she got some schooling and attended church. She was popular among the other children in the settlement, and the boys were already eyeing her thoughtfully. She had long red curls and blue eyes that turned to stormy gray whenever she was angry. By the time she turned sixteen, she was the toast of the settlement. Many of the fur traders and *voyageurs* came courting at the little house that Etienne had built for his family on the edge of town.

Out of the scores of suitors for Helene's hand arose two bitter rivals—the English fur trader Luke Scarlet, a white-blond, blue-eyed fellow with a large brown mole on his right cheek, and Jean-Pierre, a dark-haired, dark-eyed French-Canadian *voyageur*. Right from the start, Etienne and Isabel knew that their daughter had fallen for the Frenchman, but she was the high-spirited daughter of a high-spirited father, and she led her beau through a mighty dance before accepting his marriage proposal. Luke was sent away with a pat on the hand and a wistful smile. He took his dismissal like a man—at least outwardly. But inside, jealousy against the successful suitor burned like a brilliant bonfire, and the Englishman began plotting against him even before the marriage vows were taken.

Helene and Jean-Pierre settled in a log cabin near her parents, and Jean-Pierre joined Etienne in his successful fur-trading business. Together, their company became the most

HELENE AND THE LOUP GAROU

profitable in La Baye, adding yet more burning coals to the fire of Luke Scarlet's hatred.

One night in early autumn, a few months after Helene's marriage, the Englishman slipped into the woods and called upon a hermit woman who was reputed to have dealings with the Devil. She quickly produced a contract binding Luke's soul to the Devil in exchange for the ability to change into a *loup-garou*—a werewolf—and Luke signed it gladly.

The witch gave the Englishman a potion to drink that burned through his veins, cramping and stretching his body until he fell on all fours in the shape of a giant white wolf with a brown spot on his muzzle in the exact place where the dark mole sat on Luke's human cheek. A moment later, he pushed himself upward and transformed easily into man-shape. When he turned to thank the old woman, he found that witch, cabin, and clearing had all disappeared, leaving him alone in the center of the dark forest. Transforming back into a wolf, Luke ran home, rejoicing in his new senses and the ease with which he had adapted to his new shape. It was hard to think of anything but the glorious smells and the lust for blood when he was in wolf-shape; but as a man, his head was clear, and he carefully made his plan.

One afternoon in late November, while Etienne and Jean-Pierre were out checking the trap line, the dark-eyed young man bashfully told his father-in-law that he and Helene were expecting a child. The grandfather-to-be lit up like a firecracker, thumping his son-in-law on the back and exclaiming over and over again in delight. Neither of them noticed the large white wolf crouched on top of the ridge until it leapt down upon Jean-Pierre, knocking him to the ground in one terrible, graceful movement. Jean-Pierre's astonished shout was cut off abruptly as the huge white beast with one dark patch on its muzzle ripped out his throat. Etienne, frozen in astonishment, came to his senses and grabbed his gun. The wolf sprang away at once, and Etienne fired a shot after it. By the time he reloaded, it was gone.

Etienne dropped to his knees beside his son-in-law, but Jean-Pierre's eyes were already glazed over, his blood pumping out through the fatal hole where his throat used to be. Moments later, he was dead. Etienne carried the body home, so unmanned by the unexpected attack and death of his beloved son-in-law that tears streamed down his weathered cheeks in spite of his attempts to stifle them. He took the young man to his own house and sent Isabel over to the log cabin to break the news to Helene.

Helene was completely devastated, and it was only concern for her unborn child that prevented her from committing suicide. The whole community was shocked by Jean-Pierre's death. Hunting parties swiftly set out in search of the white wolf with the dark patch on its muzzle. But it was not to be found.

Luke Scarlet took the lead in the wolf hunts and was a tower of strength for Helene and her family in the first dark days following the death of Jean-Pierre. Slowly, as the winter months passed, Helene turned more and more to Luke for comfort and help. She had moved back home after her husband's death, but she still went to the log cabin once a month to make sure all was well. Her parents were sure that she would move back into her own home with a new English husband soon after the baby was born.

And so might she might have. But one evening, when Luke departed into the lightly falling snow following his daily courting call, Helene—in the manner of all expectant mothers—found it necessary to slip outside to use the privy. As she maneuvered through the snowflakes, she noticed that Luke's human footprints ended a yard or so away from the house and were replaced by the footprints of a large wolf. She lifted the lantern high and examined them carefully; sure she had made a mistake. But she had not.

All the way to the privy and back, Helene thought about what she had seen. And her speculations were not pleasant. A lone wolf with white fur and a brown patch on its muzzle had killed her husband. And now her English suitor—with his white-blond hair and the dark mole on his cheek—had seemingly turned into a wolf upon his departure from her home. *Loup-garou*, she thought, her blue eyes turning to a stormy gray that boded ill for her suitor.

Helene behaved in her normal fashion the next evening when Luke came to call. But she slipped to the window and watched as he departed from her parent's home. A few yards from the house, he transformed into a large white wolf with a dark patch on its muzzle and bounded lightly into the trees in the direction of his home.

"Papa," Helene said the next morning over breakfast. "I saw the white wolf last night roaming near our house."

Her words brought an instant silence to the table. Isabel's fork hung halfway between her plate and her mouth. Etienne stopped chewing for a moment and then swallowed convulsively.

"The white wolf? Here?" he asked incredulously. "After all this time?"

"I do not think it is an ordinary wolf, Papa," Helene said meaningfully, jerking her chin toward the family Bible that sat on a corner table. Etienne's eyes widened as he caught her meaning. Not one of God's creatures, acting out of hunger and instinct, but a shape-changer who refused to say Mass and had contracted with the Devil.

"A *loup-garou* then," Etienne said slowly, nodding in agreement. He had wondered himself if this was not so, since the creature had appeared so suddenly when it killed Jean-Pierre and had disappeared so thoroughly afterward.

Isabel gasped. "Oh, Helene! Surely not. Why would a *loup-garou* kill Jean-Pierre?"

"You mean why would a white *loup-garou* with a dark patch on its muzzle kill Jean-Pierre?" asked Helene, emphasizing the creature's description. Understanding dawned on her parents' faces and then hardened immediately into anger.

Etienne fingered his gray-streaked beard thoughtfully. "Do you still have that silver tea set from your *grandmère?*" he asked his wife. She nodded, narrowing her eyes in understanding. "I will fetch it at once," she said, putting down her serviette and hurrying away from the table.

Etienne spent the day melting silver and making bullets for his rifle. That evening, he left the house a few minutes before Luke arrived, carrying both his rifle and the shiny new gun that had once belonged to Jean-Pierre. When Luke questioned his absence, the women told him that Etienne had gone out to do some nighttime hunting. They did not tell the Englishman what sort of creature he was hunting, and he did not think to ask.

After spending an hour or so teasing the fair Helene about possible names for her new child, which he swore would be a son, Luke finally drew on his coat, bade his sweetheart and her mother goodnight, and left the house. Helene and Isabel stayed beside the warm fire, watching it snap and sizzle in the hearth and listening . . . listening . . .

Five minutes later, they heard the sharp report of her father's rifle, followed swiftly by a second shot from Jean-Pierre's gun. And then Etienne came back to the house, dragging the corpse of a large white wolf with a brown patch on its cheek.

The next morning, the family took the wolf into town to show all the settlers that the murderous creature had been killed at last. Folks gathered around to see and exclaim over the wolf, and several fur-traders offered to buy it from Etienne so that they could sell its lovely white fur. But Etienne refused to sell the wolf, and folks assumed he was going to make a rug out of it for his widowed daughter. Instead, he took it outside of town and buried it deep in the woods.

It wasn't until much later that the townsfolk realized that Luke Scarlet had disappeared. But they never associated his disappearance with the death of the white wolf. Most folks reckoned he'd been turned down again by Helene and had left town to save face. Etienne's family was content to let them think so.

No one in La Baye ever learned the true story until so many years had passed that all the key characters were long since gone to Glory. It was Helene's son—named Jean-Pierre, for his father—who finally passed the tale down to his grandchildren, and it is still told to this day.

17

The Dark Lord's Curse

It was Johnny Inkslinger, the camp clerk, who first noticed there was a problem. He had just refilled the twenty-gallon tank of ink that he drained daily in his effort to keep up with the records for Paul Bunyan's logging camp when he was called away from his desk in the wanigan—that is, the store—to sell about a thousand shirts to the ten thousand new loggers who'd joined the camp for the winter. As soon as he could, Johnny hurried back to his desk. He loved figures (he'd invented accounting and bookkeeping right around the time Paul Bunyan invented logging), and he couldn't bear to be away from his books for more than an hour or so at a time.

Johnny picked up three pens in each hand, nodded to his pet mouse to stand ready to roll across the desk and blot paper as soon as he was finished with each sheet, and prepared to add up the wanigan intake log in one hand while he subtracted the expenses with the other. And that's when he realized that his newly filled tank of ink was empty.

Now, someone other than Johnny Inkslinger might have thought that they'd made a mistake and hadn't really refilled the twenty-gallon inkwell before the sudden rush on new shirts.

But Johnny didn't make mistakes like that. He had a keen head on his shoulders—which was why he was so good at sums—and he knew without a doubt that he'd just refilled the giant inkwell. He had the stains on his fingers to prove it. So what had happened to all the ink?

Johnny searched the hoses for kinks and found none. Then he looked into the barrel. It was empty. He checked the barrel for leaks. There were none. He concluded that someone was playing a very nasty joke on him. But how? The accounting area was always kept locked when he was working at the counter of the wanigan, since Johnny wouldn't tolerate anyone touching his ledgers. (Besides, you couldn't be too careful in a logging camp that employed ten thousand lumberjacks.) The only key was the one in Johnny's waistcoat pocket, and it was still in its place. Johnny shook his head. The ink must have been stolen through magic means. There was no other way.

To test his theory, he got ink from the supplies—carefully noting (in pencil) that he was required to use more ink than usual on this particular day—and started pouring the ink into the barrel. It settled in the bottom for a moment. Then a hole magically appeared and the ink started to swirl and drain out of the barrel. As soon as it was gone, the hole disappeared again with a small pop. Ah, ha! Someone had cursed the logging camp's giant inkwell! Johnny got rid of the bedeviled barrel, filled a new one with ink, and went back to his records. But all the rest of the day, he thought about the curse. Was it against him personally, or against the whole camp? he wondered. He decided to investigate.

After carefully putting away his ledgers, and setting a lucky rabbit's foot on top of the new ink barrel—hoping this would discourage more curses—Johnny filled up his pockets with some of his personal lucky charms and sacred relicts and made a note to himself to order several hundred more to sell in the camp wanigan (five for a dollar) to anyone else suffering from the curse. Then he went searching for some of the other bosses in the lumber camp. He ran Sourdough Sam down in the giant cooking shanty, which was half a mile long and took about a day to walk around. It was lined with long tables and benches. At one end was a cooking range several acres in length that required three-fourths of forest to be cut every day just to keep it lit.

Sourdough Sam was hopping on one foot and waving his crutch in the air in annoyance at an under-chef as Johnny Inkslinger approached. Sam had lost his leg in a sourdough explosion shortly after his romance with a witch-woman had gone bad, back in the north woods of Michigan last season. He didn't miss it much, since it didn't interfere with his ability to cook meals for Paul Bunyan or the other loggers.

"I said fifty bushels of potatoes, not fifteen!" the cook howled at his underling, who turned red and hurried away to peel another thirty-five bushels of potatoes for supper. "It's so hard to get good help these days," Sourdough moaned to Johnny Inkslinger.

Johnny nodded sympathetically and then said: "Say, Sam, have you noticed anything strange happening lately in the cooking shanty?"

Sam perked up immediately. "I'll say! The wood doesn't burn as hot as it used to. Sometimes the fire goes out completely, even though a new cord of wood has just been added to it. And the flames near the bottom of the fire—the ones that should be hottest—feel icy cold! Reminds me a bit of that time the witch-woman cursed my stove last season." Sam went pale and shuddered suddenly. Clutching Johnny's arm, he said: "You don't think she's come back, do you?"

Johnny Inkslinger shook his head. "She's happily married to an old hermit now and serving him possum stew morning, noon, and night," he reported. Both men made faces at the thought. "But I do think something supernatural is going on around here, and I aim to figure out what it is."

Johnny sold Sourdough Sam a lucky rabbit's foot for a quarter and told him to put it on the range. "You'll probably need more than one to lift the curse on a half-acre range," he told the cook. "I'm putting in a big order for sacred relics and lucky charms. You may want to reserve a few for the cooking shanty. I have a feeling they're going to go fast."

Sourdough Sam immediately ordered about a hundred more rabbit feet and another fifty lucky pendants, just in case. Satisfied, Johnny Inkslinger continued his wanderings through Paul Bunyan's logging camp, searching for more evidence of a curse.

Johnny Inkslinger was more than fifty feet from the barn when a string of cusswords came bursting forth, blistering the bark of the surrounding trees and melting the snow right out from under his feet. Johnny picked up his pace with a grin. Obviously Brimstone Bill, the camp's boss bullwhacker—what most folks call an animal keeper—was in residence. Brimstone had invented just about every cussword known to man and had written the *Skinner's Dictionary*, an international bestseller on the best cusswords and torrid terms to use when driving oxen. Brimstone Bill had dedicated the book to Babe the Blue Ox and his cousin Little Benny, who had inspired him. He'd gone on to write several more instructional books for sailors, bartenders, and other folk who needed to know how to cuss effectively. He was considered the world expert on the subject.

When Johnny entered the barn, he saw a brawny man with a red face and a long white beard wearing a slouch hat, a red flannel shirt, blue jumpers, and big black boots. He was face to snout with Little Benny, who was a rambunctious little ox ten times bigger than Brimstone, though only half the size of Babe. Little Benny had kicked a huge hole in the wall of his stall and was trying to buck his way out of it. Brimstone had had a ring drilled through the ornery critter's nose as soon as he realized what a rascal Little Benny was, and he was clinging to the ring with both hands, trying to keep the ox from running away.

Brimstone was nearly halfway through his list of ten thousand cusswords, with Little Benny trying hard to toss him through the rafters, when they both caught sight of Johnny Inkslinger. Forgetting their quarrel, they rushed over to greet their friend. Johnny said "howdy" to Brimstone, slipped Benny a couple of apples that he kept in his satchel, and got on with his investigation.

"Strange dad-blame things going on, you say?" asked Brimstone, toning down his usual cussing on account of Johnny being an educated chap. "We've got a list as long as your dad-blame arm, don't we, Little Benny?"

The blue ox snorted and stamped in agreement.

"Take a look at Little Benny's gosh-darn hooves, for Pete's sake," said Brimstone, sweating a little since it was so hard not to cuss in front of Johnny. "Them ox shoes keep falling off every ding-dang-dong day."

Johnny bent down to look at the shoes. Yes indeed, they were loose. The one he was studying came off in his hand.

Brimstone Bill let out a string of cusswords that nearly burned off the tips of Johnny's ears.

"Oops! Sorry about that, Johnny," Brimstone said sheepishly. "It's just that Ole Olson put them shoes on only yesterday!"

"He's definitely suffering from a curse," Johnny said, rubbing his burning ears. "A very expensive curse, too, if it means making new shoes every day!"

Johnny Inkslinger was becoming annoyed. This curse was costing the camp good money, and he didn't like to see profits going down the drain. He handed a lucky penny to the boss bullwhacker. "You'd better keep this lucky penny tied around Little Benny's neck," said Johnny. "I'm putting in a big order for talismans, amulets, and sacred relics. I'll put you down for a cartload."

"Have you got another lucky penny or two?" asked Brimstone. "Babe's losing his shoes too."

Johnny handed him a second lucky penny and went to visit Ole Olson, the blacksmith. The heat coming from the smithy was nearly as powerful as Brimstone Bill at his worst. There was no snow for almost a hundred feet around the building, and Johnny could see where Ole's footprints had sunk deep into solid rock when he'd carried Babe's heavy shoes to the stable. That had been the first time Ole shoed the big blue ox. After that, Babe had come to the smithy whenever he needed new shoes.

Ole was forging some new chains for the heavy sledges used to haul logs when Johnny arrived. Behind him ticked the massive pocket watch that the King of Sweden had given Paul Bunyan as a gift.

"Howdy, Ole. Watch need repairing again?" asked Johnny. Once a year, Ole took the watch apart, greased up the parts, and made sure everything was in working order. Whenever the watch was taken apart, it made a large labyrinth behind the smithy. The first year it was repaired, several lumberjacks had gotten lost inside the works, and it took Ole three days to find them. After that, Ole set up danger signs all around the watch-labyrinth to keep people out.

"'Tis the strangest thing, Yohnny," Ole said in his soft Swedish accent. He laid aside his huge hammer and rubbed his chin in distress. "Ze pocket watch, zhe has always run smoothly, but now zhe need repairing almost every day. Me, I must take her apart to fix, I think. But alas, I cannot do zo right now, because there are zo many other repairs to da camp."

"More repairs then usual?" asked Johnny sharply.

"Ya! Many more repairs this season," said Ole glumly. "You know, Yohnny, I think this camp is under a curse."

"I think you are right," said Johnny.

Just then, Sourdough Sam blew the supper horn. Ole closed down the forge, and both men went to the massive dining hall for dinner. On the way, Johnny told Ole all he knew about the curse.

"You vill have to tell the boss, no?" said Ole.

"Yes, it's time to tell the boss," said Johnny Inkslinger.

As Ole took a spot at one of the huge wooden tables, Johnny went over to the massive head table near the half-acre range where Paul Bunyan sat buttering a stack of pancakes that reached nearly as high as the ceiling. Twelve "cookies"—assistant cooks—were running back and forth with new batches of syrup and butter and pancakes trying to keep him fed. Johnny slid into a chair beside him and cleared his throat several times before Paul Bunyan heard him and moved the giant bottle of maple syrup so he could see him. An assistant cook thrust a plate full of flapjacks in front of Johnny Inkslinger.

"How's business in the wanigan?" Paul Bunyan asked jovially as he forked another ten flapjacks into his mouth.

"Not good, boss," said Johnny, taking a bite out of his stack of pancakes. "Somebody's put a curse on the logging camp, and it's going to cost us a bundle if we don't put a stop to it right away."

"What do you mean, a curse?" asked Paul Bunyan, frowning down at his clerk. Johnny started at the beginning and explained everything he'd seen and heard that afternoon.

Paul Bunyan chewed on the news as he chewed on his flapjacks. "Can't be that witch-woman that was hankering after Sourdough last season," he said at last. "She's happily wed to that hermit fellow. Must be someone else. Find out who, Johnny, and I'll put a stop to it. Meantime, we'd better stock up on lucky rabbits' feet and amulets and such."

"Will do, boss," said Johnny, finishing up his flapjacks. "There's one thing I have noticed. Most of the pranks seem to come from down near the ground. The bottom of the barrel, the oxen's feet, the bottom of the fire burning cold."

"Think we've offended some sort of Indian Manitou who lives under the forest?"

"I dunno," said Johnny Inkslinger. "I'm going to find out before the camp goes broke."

Johnny marched back to the wanigan and sent a messenger out with an order for a couple thousand amulets, lucky charms, holy relics, and other talismans. The next morning, he rounded up several of the local tribesmen to find out which of their gods lived in the area, and if any of them might be offended by the work of the lumberjacks. Everyone he interviewed was stumped by the situation. The logging camp wasn't violating any sacred ground, and none of the medicine men had any sign that their gods were offended in any way. Johnny was frustrated. How in tarnation was he going to find out who was at the bottom of the trouble?

Meanwhile, strange things kept happening in the camp. One day the cook stove fire would burn so hot that the food would get burnt, and the next day they could barely keep the fire going and all the food would be soggy. Barrels and hoops and chains and all sorts of ironwork would rust or crack or get holes and need repairing. Of course, Ole had no time to fix any of them, since none of the oxen could keep their shoes on. The lucky amulets helped somewhat, and soon every man in the camp was covered head to toe with lucky rabbits' feet, holy relics, and so many chains that the clatter and chiming they made when they moved drowned out the sound of the saws and the thud of the falling trees.

Some days, the men would get lost on their way to the privy, even though it was only twenty feet from the bunkhouse. Other days, the lumberjacks would spend all morning piling and chaining fifty logs onto a sleigh, only to have the chains snap near the bottom as soon as the last log was loaded. Off the logs would tumble, and the men had to dive out of the way or be crushed to death. Then the men had to collect the scattered logs and pile them on again.

Sometimes the oxen or horses would strain and strain against a load and it wouldn't budge, even when it was sitting on slippery ice. Then it would suddenly come loose and knock the oxen head over heels. By the end of February, only Babe and Little Benny could reliably haul logs down to the river, where they were stacked into rollaways—piles of logs ready to be pushed into the river when it thawed in the spring. Once, all the boards holding the rollaways in place broke at the same moment, and the logs tumbled down onto the frozen river. The men spent quite a number of hours putting them back into place, and Brimstone Bill was banished to the bunkhouse for fear he would start cussing and melt the river before the men could retrieve all the logs.

Johnny Inkslinger was in a terrible state. The logging camp was losing money to the curse, lumberjacks were quitting left and right, and Paul Bunyan kept shouting: "Johnny, find me the dad-blame person responsible for this curse!" every night at dinner. The first time he shouted at Johnny, the roof flipped end over end and landed on top of the barn. It took fifty men to fetch it down, and Ole had to make special iron bands to keep it in place when Paul shouted.

"I'm going to have to call in some special help," Johnny told Paul Bunyan glumly as they watched the ice floes slowly breaking up in the river. "I'm going to go visit that witch-woman that Sourdough Sam jilted and see if she can divine who put a curse on us. If I don't, we probably won't be able to get our logs to market."

Johnny didn't like leaving the wanigan in the hands of an assistant, but he felt he had no choice. Paul Bunyan couldn't go himself because he was taking the first load of logs downriver to the sawmill—he was afraid something strange might happen on the way because of the curse, and he wanted to oversee the operation himself. Besides, he'd asked Johnny to find out who'd made the curse, so it looked like the task was his. So Johnny

THE DARK LORD'S CURSE

loaded the boss up with every charm he had left in the wanigan, and as Paul Bunyan rode the logs south, he traveled east to the home of the witch-woman.

A half-day's ride put Johnny into the woods near the witch-woman's home. She came eagerly out to greet him and proudly displayed the gnarled little hermit-man who was her husband. Over possum stew, Johnny told the witch about the troubles the camp had been having all winter. As soon as she ascertained the fact that Johnny was full and didn't want any more stew, the witch poured ink into a saucer and began scrying in search of the person who had cursed the camp.

First she called up several pictures of the logging camp. Johnny saw men felling trees, Brimstone hauling them away on his sleigh, and Ole Olson putting the finishing touches on Paul Bunyan's watch, which was finally fixed.

The pictures in the ink changed to that of Paul Bunyan and his men riding the logs south toward the sawmill. Or were they going south? The witch-woman tutted softly to herself. "There's something strange about that river," she told Johnny. "It's been cursed." She waved her hand over the ink, and the picture changed to a birds-eye view of the landscape. Looking down, Johnny could see that the river was completely round. Paul Bunyan and the men riding the logs were going around and around in a large circle and getting nowhere!

"That's a pretty bad curse," said the witch. "Let's see who made it."

The pictures in the ink started flickering by so fast that they made Johnny dizzy, and he had to look away.

"There he is," the witch-woman said at last, and Johnny looked back into the saucer. Sitting deep under the water, in a strange little kingdom of seaweed and sunken ships, was a dark-eyed, dark-skinned Manitou god with a long fish tail instead of legs. He had a cruel smile on his face and was watching Paul Bunyan and his men riding in circles in a little mirror propped before his rocky underwater throne.

"Who's that?" he asked the witch.

"That's Matchi Manitou, Lake Superior's water god," she replied. "No wonder all the curses seemed to affect the bottom of things instead of the top. He must have been sending them up from the bottom of the lake. Matchi Manitou is a nasty one. Most of the tribesmen hereabouts drop trinkets and other offerings in the water to appease him whenever they travel across the lake. I wonder what happened to make him curse your lumber camp?"

"I have no idea," said Johnny. "But I'd better ride back right away, get Paul off that round river if I can, and see if we can't parlay with the water god."

The witch-woman was disappointed. "My husband and I were hoping you'd stay to supper," she said. But Johnny was in a hurry to get back and soon was speeding away on his horse.

Johnny Inkslinger reached camp at the same time as Paul Bunyan and his men finally broke free of the round river. Paul ordered about a hundred lumberjacks to stand beside the river and catch the logs on their next trip around so they could haul them away to another river. Then he strode up to Johnny, his eyes sparkling with rage.

"Who's behind this curse?" he demanded without preamble.

"The Lake Superior water god," said Johnny at once.

"Why?" roared Paul.

"I don't know," said Johnny. "Why don't we ask?"

With a shout of rage that blew over a dozen trees, Paul Bunyan strode north until he reached the edge of the lake. Using his axe like a spoon, he began stirring the lake up until huge waves formed, knocking things around clear to the bottom of the lake. It didn't take long for the dark-eyed water god to appear on the surface of the lake, fish tail thrashing. He rose out of the giant waves, growing larger with each slap of his tail until he was as tall as Paul Bunyan.

"Why do you disturb my Lake?" he shouted.

"Why do you curse my lumber camp?" Paul Bunyan shouted back.

"Because you stole my favorite sea serpent and threw him into the ocean," roared Matchi Manitou. "Bring him back at once, or I will flood your whole camp until each and every one of you drowns."

"Is that what all this fuss is about?" Paul Bunyan asked, calming down at once. "You should have said so. That pesky sea serpent of yours tried to eat Babe the Blue Ox last season. He deserved what he got."

"I want him back," howled the water god, his dark eyes filling with tears like a spoiled little boy. "Bring him back right now."

"I'll bring him back to you if you promise he won't pester Babe any more," Paul Bunyan said sternly.

Matchi Manitou promised to keep the sea serpent away from the lumber camp if Paul Bunyan would return him to Lake Superior. He even gave the massive lumberjack a special whistle he used to call the serpent so that it would be easier to retrieve him from the ocean.

Happy now that his pet was to be returned, the water god went back under the lake. Paul Bunyan left Brimstone Bill and Johnny Inkslinger in charge of the lumber camp and went west to the Pacific Ocean to retrieve the sea serpent he'd flung there last season after it attacked Babe the Blue Ox.

Within a month, the sea serpent was back where it belonged, and it was a much humbler and wiser sea serpent after its sojourn in the depths of the Pacific. So the water god removed the curse from the lumber camp, Johnny Inkslinger went back to his ledgers, and Paul Bunyan got all the promised lumber down to the sawmill in time, which made everybody happy.

18

The House-Troll

MOUNT HOREB

Snip-snap-spin,
Our story begins . . .

It was a foolproof operation. They were thieves with an ace up the sleeve that no one—not even in their wildest dreams—would have guessed. The husband descended from a long line of thieves and rogues who lived atop a fell in Norway. Long ago, the family had contracted with the trolls who lived within the mountain to aid and abet their thieving in exchange for gold. The wife came from a respectable family that had secretly kept a family of small trolls bound to them as slaves, ordering them to do all the work around the house and farm while the humans lounged about, growing fatter and lazier with each succeeding generation.

The couple took the show on the road, traveling to visit friends, family, distant relations, and friends of friends all over the world with a special suitcase containing a secret compartment in which a small house-troll made itself at home during the nasty daytime hours when it could turn to stone in the light of the sun, and from which it roamed freely at night, stealing jewelry and money and other easy-to-hide dainties that brought a tidy sum when sold on the black market. Best of all, no one suspected. After all, in this enlightened age, no one believed in trolls. They were just a fanciful myth from old Norway. According to the legends, the Earth was created from the corpse of a giant called Ymir, and trolls were the transformed dark spirits of maggots that emerged from the decaying body. Trolls were evil creatures, some big and some small, who lived underground during the day and came out at night to steal and plot mischief and sometimes prey upon the humans living in the world above them.

It took some time for anyone to begin connecting the couple with the thefts. Most of the relatives and friends thought they had mislaid the missing items, and guests were too embarrassed to report the disappeared items to the police.

"Cannot find your wallet, *venn?*" the husband would say sympathetically. "Maybe the trolls got it, ho-ho!"

The guests would chuckle, and the "friend" would flush and say that he must have put the wallet in his other jacket.

"A missing ring? Tut, tut!" said the wife. "My *bestemor*— you know, my grandmother—was always losing her rings, too. She said the trolls stole them. Ho-ho! But they always turned up again in the bread dough or under the bed."

"Ho-ho!" chuckled the relatives. No one believed in trolls.

If something expensive was stolen, the couple was always first in line to help look for it. They insisted upon having their room searched as an example for the other guests. The house-troll used a special sort of magic to conceal the secret compartment, so no one ever found it or suspected that the couple had a small troll sleeping inside with a ruby necklace clutched tight in his tiny claws.

Still, enough incidents happened that friends and relatives on the Continent became suspicious. The police interviewed the couple a few times, but they never found anything. The couple knew they were being closely watched, so they decided to try their luck somewhere else. They had never been to America and decided that this was a good time to visit the New World. They flew to Wisconsin to visit a fourth-cousin-once-removed, and soon were driving with their host toward a nice home outside of town.

"I see you like trolls, ho-ho," chuckled the husband to his host as they drove along Main Street. He gestured to the wooden statues of trolls scattered through the downtown area.

"We sure do, ho-ho," responded the fourth-cousin-once-removed. "A local artist—chap name Mike Finney—carves them. They're something of a fad with us."

"Ever seen the real thing?" asked the husband jovially.

The fourth-cousin-once-removed laughed uproariously. "Not yet!" he gasped happily. "Not yet!"

The couple chuckled with their host and settled back against their seats to enjoy the ride. This would be easy! Deep inside the trunk, the house-troll stirred a bit when it heard the loud laughter and then went back to sleep.

While the couple was having a late dinner with their host and hostess, the little house-troll was happily exploring his new surroundings. He was a small Old World troll who resembled a pig with pointed ears, a small snout, and little pinkish eyes. He had two tails that wagged back and forth as he walked, and he wore a formal bunad costume, part of the deal his family had struck long ago with the family of the wife whom they served in the Old World. The little troll found it itchy and uncomfortable, but slaves have no choice in the matter.

Scratching himself in a not-so-nice way, he nicked a few strands of pearls from the wife's dressing table, stole some loose change from the husband's wallet, and then nipped out into the darkness for a walk. He dashed hither and thither through the balmy summer night, checking doors and crawling in and out of open windows. Several times he returned to the house to empty his little sack into the secret compartment before heading out again.

The little house-troll finally wandered onto the Main Street of the nearby town. In the moonlight, he spotted a tall figure carrying a parasol. He blinked a few times in the dim light from the crescent moon and then gave a happy whistle. It was one of the huldrafolk, no mistake.

"Ho-ho, me proud beauty," he called excitedly in Norwegian, scrambling atop the tall stump on which she posed. "Let's scamper about in the moonlight! There's a loose windowpane in a house over yonder, and I smelled candy inside the kitchen!"

The huldra ignored him. She didn't even blink or turn her head. The little house-troll was annoyed. The first troll he'd seen in months, and she was ignoring him. Playing hard to get, he decided, dropping back down to the ground. Well, two could play that game. Besides, she was too tall anyway. He liked smaller troll-females. They were cuddlier. And after all, the huldra had only one tail. A fine house-troll like him needed to have standards.

He raced away down the street and almost collided with a large stump on the sidewalk. Jumping back a little, the house-troll gazed upward at a jolly-looking fellow with an accordion. The house-troll jumped up and down excitedly.

"Play some *musikk, venn!*" he called. The troll stood silent and still atop his stump. The little house-troll called again to him, but he didn't answer. Both of the house-troll's tails twitched back and forth in annoyance at the rude behavior of the troll.

THE HOUSE-TROLL

Of course, all trolls were rude to one another, but none of the trolls living in Norway would completely ignore a fellow. Belt him one, maybe. Shout curses at him, definitely. But never the silent treatment. Who did they think they were anyway, these New World trolls?

Away the house-troll trotted down the street, as mad as could be. He was so steamed up, he forgot to watch the time. The sky above him was changing color, becoming gray instead of black, and birds were beginning to chirp. Then his keen nose caught the smell of chickens not too far away, and the rude American trolls were forgotten in an instant. With the uncanny speed for which house-trolls were known, he trotted down the road toward the smell. A farmhouse loomed out of the darkness, and behind it was a barn and . . . ah-ha! . . . a chicken coop.

The sky was pearly gray as the house-troll swarmed up the chicken-wire fence and leapt to the top of the coop. He gave a little dance of joy. He was going to eat fresh chicken! Hurrah! It was at that moment that the first rays of the sun came up over the horizon and all the birds burst into happy song. And the little house-troll turned to stone right on top of the hen-house roof.

When the farmer came to feed the hens a few minutes later, he saw a large knobby rock sitting on top of the chicken coop. If you looked closely at it, it was shaped a bit like a pig wearing a bonad, with two long dark bumps that might have been two tails. But the farmer didn't look too closely.

"I wish these kids would stop fooling around in the chicken coop," he fussed. The farmer tossed the heavy little rock over the fence. It rolled under a bush and disappeared from sight.

The couple didn't miss their house-troll. Their policy was to completely ignore the troll and its antics until they were safely back home in Norway. Only then would they unpack the secret compartment to see what it had stolen for them.

The couple stayed for a week with their fourth-cousins-once-removed and then went to the airport to fly to South America for a visit with a friend of a friend. But their baggage didn't make it through the safety check at the airport. Without the troll's magic, the secret compartment was readily visible to the electronic scanners.

The thieving couple was taken aside by security, the stolen goods were found, and the two were arrested. When the husband and wife protested that it was a troll that had stolen all the money and jewelry found inside the secret compartment in their luggage, they were committed to a psychiatric ward under heavy guard. It became their permanent home after the trial.

After this incident, no one else in the family of thieves ever tried taking a troll abroad again.

Snip-snap-spout.
This story's told out.

19

The Kobold Toymaker

I was eight years old when we left *Köln* in what is present-day Germany to come to Wisconsin. *Mein Vater,* he came from a noble family and was expected to follow in his father's footsteps. But his father was stern and cruel, and they could never agree. After one particularly fierce argument with his parents, *Vater* sold everything we had, packed up the family, and left on the first boat he could find for America. We had kinfolk in Wisconsin who would help us make a new start.

The ocean journey took more than a month. I was seasick at first, and homesick for my pretty house and my dolls, but we were no longer a noble family, *Mein Vater* told me. We were Americans now, and we could not afford to have pretty things until we earned them for ourselves. But my three brothers and I soon made friends with the other children on board, and when the weather was fair, we would laugh and play together while our parents visited with other families on deck. Sometimes they would make music and we would all dance.

I didn't like the stormy days in the hold of the ship, with everyone packed together like sardines in a tin. And some of the children got sick. Mama kept us away from the sick ones, fearing we would become ill. But my five-year-old brother got measles—he was the only one of us who had not had them before we left *Köln*. He died on that voyage, as did twelve other children. It was a very sad beginning to our new life in America.

Mein Vater knew precisely what to do when we got to New York, for his cousin had written him a letter telling him how to get to Wisconsin. We hurried past the men trying to sell us things we did not need—*con men, Vater* called them—and went to the office of a steam boat to book passage up the Hudson River, through the Erie Canal, and onto a ship that would take us across the Great Lakes to Milwaukee. The trip took us ten days.

The cousin of *Mein Vater* met us in Milwaukee and took us to his farm in Sheboygan County. The money *Vater* had made selling our possessions was enough to buy us land, and we stayed with our cousins while the other German men in our settlement erected a small farmhouse and a barn for us. We loved our new home, my brothers and I. We had lived in the city all our lives, and so life on a farm was very new and very wonderful to us.

Most of *Vater*'s money had gone into the purchase of the land and the equipment needed to farm it. We had little left over for the luxuries that we'd left behind. But we took delight in the two cows and the hens given to us by our cousin, and we explored the woods surrounding our wheat fields when the chores were done. We learned to milk and gather eggs. Mama, who had never worked a day in her life, now learned to churn butter and cook and make a garden, with the help of her new friends from the Lutheran church in town. Her soft white hands grew brown and calloused, but she was still the same sweet Mama, and she never complained of her loss of status or of the labor she now endured for the sake of *Vater*'s dream.

Vater grew wheat, like our cousin. In the fall a machine went from farm to farm to help thresh the farmer's wheat. Mama cooked up a great feast for all the men who came to help *Vater* when it was our turn to use the threshing machine.

We had enough food for winter, and warm—if plain—clothes to wear. But the crop our first year was small. *Vater* would have to cut down many more trees to have large wheat fields like those of his cousins. He would cut down the trees during the winter and sell the lumber at the local sawmill, and in spring we would all help root out the stumps to make a new field for *Vater*'s wheat.

We settled down for a long, cold winter with much help from the cousins. We really knew so little about living off the land that first year. Mama announced early in November that there would be no presents this year for Saint Nicholas Day. Every penny had gone into buying coal and flour and other supplies for the long Wisconsin winter. But she would prepare a big dinner for us to eat and be merry with, and perhaps *Vater* would earn enough next year for us to exchange gifts.

Of the many shocks my brothers and I had received during that year of transition to a new life, this was the worst. We had always had elaborate celebrations for Saint Nicholas Day back at home. Parades and feasts, visits from *Der Belznickel* to make sure we had been good children all year, and on the night of December 5, we would put our shoes by the front door. In the morning, our shoes would be filled up with fruits and nuts, and many gifts would surround each one. Mostly the gifts were from Mama and *Vater*, but I had always believed a few were from Saint Nicholas himself or one of his kobold toymakers.

Mama put on a brave face for us when she talked about Saint Nicholas Day, but we knew—my brothers and I—that she was ashamed to be so poor that she had nothing to give her children. Not even a few pennies left over for store-bought candy. That first year on the frontier, she knew none of the little tricks that the other farm wives used to make toys and candy from what little they had. She'd had enough difficulty just learning the things she must in order for us to survive.

My brothers and I decided to make gifts for one another, and we went searching around the barn and the woods and the house for leftover bits and pieces to use in their construction. During the summer I had grown out of the last of my pretty clothes from my old life, and they had been packed away at the bottom of my little trunk. I dug out a pretty white linen frock and a thick velvet one and took them up to the garret with my little scissors and my sewing kit to try to come up with something creative to make for my family.

As I sat staring at the pretty fabrics, I heard a small tap-tap-tapping sound coming from the far corner. I looked around, and there was a tiny little man in a close-fitting brown jacket with a cap—what we call a *zipfelkappen*—on top of his tiny head. There was a tassel on the end of it, and the little nose above his long white beard was shiny red at the tip. He sat on a small stool, tapping away at a long leather object he held in his hands. It looked like a new shoe, just the size for Frederick, my eldest brother. The shoes he brought from our old home were too small now and had holes in them.

I stared at the little man with my mouth hanging open in surprise. It was a kobold toymaker. One of Saint Nicholas's helpers— at least, that was the story my nanny told me back in *Köln*.

"Mind your manners, *Mädchen*," he said gruffly when he noticed my staring. "If you are going to share the garret with me, then do so quietly. I have much work to do before the Feast."

I nodded, unable to speak, and turned back to my sewing. I decided to make handkerchiefs for my brothers and father, fashioned from the too-small white linen dress, and a pretty collar for my mother, made from the blue velvet. I set to work, staying near the window to make the most of the winter sunlight. On the other side of the garret, the tap-tapping sound changed. I glanced over and saw that the toymaker was carving something from a slab of wood. It looked like a wooden train for my middle brother, Klaus, to play with.

When the light faded, I went downstairs to help Mama with supper. I didn't mention the kobold. My parents and Frederick didn't believe in fairy tales. When Klaus and I were doing the dishes, I told him what I had seen in the garret. His eyes popped out in amazement, and when the last dish was dried, we crept upstairs and peeked inside. From the far corner, there came a tap-tap-tapping sound, and we saw the little kobold working by the light of a tiny candle.

"Nosy children will get coal in their shoes," he snapped, without turning his head from his task. Giggling in amazement, we scurried away.

Vater and Mama looked up from their reading as we settled down to study near the warm stove. They smiled at our bright faces and listened to us recite our lessons. It was three days until Saint Nicholas Day and suddenly, I couldn't wait!

I spent every spare minute working on the handkerchiefs and velvet collar, but I didn't return to the garret for fear the kobold would leave without finishing his Saint Nicholas Day gifts. I had brought some embroidery thread with me from our old home, and so I made a fancy blue edging for each handkerchief and

THE KOBOLD TOYMAKER

put my father's initials on one of them, and Frederick's and Klaus's initials on the others. Then I sewed up the pretty velvet collar for Mama, and my gifts were done.

After Mama and I had finished making breads and puddings and pies for the Saint Nicholas feast, and after our parents had gone to bed on December 5, my brothers and I gathered up all the shoes and put them by the front door. We laid out our presents, telling each other over and over not to peek, and then hurried off to bed. Klaus and I exchanged excited grins as we parted for the night.

The next morning, *Vater* was the first one up. His exclamation of surprise woke everyone in the house, and we all hurried to the front room, wild with excitement. There were *Vater's* work boots, filled with dried fruit and nuts and candy from the kobold. Beside the boots were several gifts, including my handkerchief, a carved bear from Frederick, a strange contraption that was for cleaning boots from Klaus, and a new leather harness for the horses, which could only have come from the kobold. *Vater* stared and stared at the new leather harness

145

that he needed so badly, for he had only been able to afford a worn-out secondhand harness when we arrived.

Mother's shoes were also filled with good things to eat, and beside them were the velvet collar, a pretty wood carving of a rabbit from Frederick, a strange contraption for cleaning the stove from Klaus, and a pile of beautiful pink lawn fabric from the kobold.

Next to the boys' shoes were the handkerchiefs and some strange-looking toys they'd invented for themselves. The kobold had left Frederick the new shoes and Klaus a beautifully carved and painted wooden train with wheels that really moved.

By my shoes were a handkerchief box carved by Frederick and a device for storing thread made by Klaus. That was all. No toys from the kobold. The place where my shoes stood looked very bare compared to the rest.

Then we heard a thump, thump, thump as heavy footsteps came down the stairs from the garret. The kobold came into the front room carrying a huge dollhouse with fancy turrets and many windows, and little shingles on the roof. Everyone stared at him in shock as he trudged over and laid the dollhouse at my feet.

"For a good *Mädchen* on Saint Nicholas Day," he said to me. Then he nodded to my parents, winked at my brothers, and disappeared in a puff of air. My parents exclaimed in surprise and delight, and everyone clustered around, admiring their gifts, until *Vater* shooed us off to do our chores and Mama went to cook our feast.

It was the very best Saint Nicholas Day we had ever had. In later years, we became prosperous, and the gifts we exchanged were store bought. We never received kobold gifts again. Just that one special year, when we had nothing to give each other but love and the things we could make with our own hands.

20

Taliesin Dreaming

The day was extremely hot, and I was grateful to feel the coolness of the air-conditioning as I mounted the steps into the little tour bus that would take me and my niece, and the rest of the tourists, over to Taliesin. Taliesin was once the home of Frank Lloyd Wright, the famous American architect, and I'm ashamed to admit I'd never been there before, in spite of living within a half hour of the estate for most of my life. But when Ellen came to visit me during her first week of summer break, I decided to rectify my negligent behavior.

Ellen planned to become an architect when she finished college. She had studied Wright's life her senior year in high school, and she was very eager to visit his home and studio. She even offered to drive (of course she did! She just got her license last month!) and to pay for the entrance fee. Naturally, I accepted. It would be interesting to learn more about our famous Wisconsin native.

The visitor center, which was also a restaurant, was another of Wright's designs. I enjoyed walking through the lovely building as we waited for the tour to begin. I'll be the first to admit that I don't know much about architecture, but I know what I like, and I liked what I was seeing. Low ceilings in some areas, high ones in others. Stone facing on some walls, but not on others. Lots and lots of windows to let in the light and the beautiful view of the river.

The short walk to the bus was like stepping into a sauna. Nearly a hundred degrees Fahrenheit, was my guess. Unusual for early June. The house was visible almost at once when we turned left onto the main road. It stood on the brow of a hill, looking as if it had sprung up naturally in that spot all on its own rather than being built there by human hands. I learned later that this effect was intentional. Wright specialized in what he called "organic architecture," meaning that he wanted his buildings to blend harmoniously with the nature surrounding them.

As the bus entered the grounds, I felt a slight chill and shivered. *The air-conditioning must be turned up too high*, I decided, rubbing my arms to rid them of their goose bumps. Ellen noticed the movement and said: "Do you want me to ask the bus driver to turn down the air?"

"No, no," I said at once. "I'm fine."

Ellen nodded her fair head and turned again to the window to gaze at the approaching building. It was Wright's teaching studio, she told me, bouncing in her seat with excitement, blue eyes sparkling. She was the first off the bus when we stopped and was halfway up the drive before I reached the front of the vehicle. As I negotiated the few steps to the ground, I was hit by a wave of heat like a furnace blast, and I caught a distinct smell of smoke. Hurrying away from the bus entrance to allow the other tourists to disembark, I started looking for the source of the smell. *Was a farmer doing some controlled burning in a field?*

Did someone have a fire burning in their fireplace? But why would they on such a hot day?

As I followed Ellen and the tour guide toward the front of the studio, I kept turning around, searching for the source of the smell. There was no smoke visible, just a slight haze and shimmer on the horizon that was typical in such heat. The tour guide was gesturing to the studio and giving us a brief lecture about its origins as a school run by Wright's aunts, which closed after a family scandal and was reopened a decade later as the Taliesin Fellowship, a school for apprentice architects. I fear I was distracted by the smell of smoke, which had grown stronger, and did not attend to her words as I should have. I was caught by surprise when the group started moving toward the door, and I had to hurry to catch up.

The smell of smoke dissipated once I was inside, so I stopped worrying that the heat might have caused a fire somewhere. I loved the light airiness of the first room we visited. According to our guide, the many glass windows were intended to allow people to interact and view the outdoors while still being protected from the elements. Each window was like a picture frame for the natural beauty outdoors. The tour guide elaborated more on the concept of organic architecture as we walked through a hallway to the studio, which was a later addition to the building. There, the guide discussed how Wright put his students to work on the run-down school. The apprentices assisted in its construction, operation, and maintenance. They quarried stone, collected sand from the nearby riverbed, mixed the mortar, cut down local trees for lumber, and learned through their mistakes. The building was still an active architectural studio, and we saw several apprentices diligently working on their projects. They ignored us as we went out onto the back lawn toward the theater.

Another blast of heat and the strong smell of burning wood met me as I entered the backyard. Ellen noticed my distraction and sidled over to me. "Are you all right?" she asked.

"Do you smell smoke?" I asked abruptly, without answering her. She sniffed the air a few times and shook her head. I shrugged then. "It's probably nothing," I said, and waved her down the hill to the low-ceilinged entrance to the theater. According to our guide, this was another of Wright's techniques. He created low ceilings in entrances and hallways, designed to encourage people to move out of them quickly and into the high-ceilinged, spacious gathering areas. *No lingering here* was the subtle message, and for the tall visitors among our group, this object was achieved.

We left the theater through the same constricted entranceway and walked back into the hot afternoon air up the path, under the archway dividing the two sections of the school and down the drive to the bus. We were accompanied all the way by the pungent smell of smoke, and occasionally I thought I heard voices screaming in the distance. I was rather frightened by now. No one else on the tour seemed to notice anything amiss.

As I entered the cool bus and sat down again beside Ellen, I started to wonder if the sensations I'd felt and the sounds I'd heard might be more of my visions of the past, rather than something actually happening now. The women in my family have all been born with psychic abilities—some stronger, some weaker. On rare occasions, my particular gift allowed me to see into the past. I started to ask Ellen if there had ever been a fire on the estate, but at that moment the tour guide began talking about Taliesin, Frank Lloyd Wright's home, and so I quieted myself to listen.

Apparently, Frank Lloyd Wright built Taliesin as a home for Martha "Mamah" Borthwick, the woman he loved but was unable to marry because his wife refused to divorce him. Borthwick and Wright lived there happily for a time while Wright worked as an architect. Unfortunately, the house burned down (ah, ha!) and many people were killed in the events surrounding the fire, including Mamah Borthwick and her children. I wondered a bit at the unusual phrasing—"killed in the events surrounding the fire"—but the tour guide was continuing her lecture as the bus passed the farm buildings and wound its way upward to the house on the brow of the hill.

Through the years, the guide explained, Wright used Taliesin as a sketch pad on which to actively try out his new ideas about living in harmony with nature. The land surrounding Taliesin was his inspiration. He regularly tore down parts of the house and built them anew. He used the ideas developed at Taliesin in his commissioned architectural projects. Apparently, the building we were approaching was Taliesin III. The house had burned to the ground twice during Wright's lifetime.

Well, I thought, that explained the smell of smoke.

We drove around the house, and the small bus parked in front to let us off. As soon as I stepped foot on the ground, I was overwhelmed by sights and smells and sounds. Terrible sounds. I staggered forward, my eyes filled with the vision of a wild-eyed man striding toward the house—this house, though it did not look the same. He was carrying a lighted torch and an axe, and the look on his face made me want to scream,

TALIESIN DREAMING

but my throat was so tight with terror that I couldn't utter a sound.

Somewhere behind the vision of the man, I could hear the tour guide calmly discussing the concepts that Wright had used when building the house. But all I could see was the man, disappearing into a building that had long since burnt to the ground. And all I could hear were horrible screams and pandemonium within— the moans of the dying—mingled with the smell of burning and the sight of the house in flames. I fainted.

I came to in the air-conditioned bus, surrounded by Ellen, the bus driver, and the tour guide. They assumed I had fainted because of the intense heat outside, and I was happy to let them think so. I remained huddled inside the bus while everyone else took the house tour. Ellen wanted to stay with me, but I insisted she go along. I would be fine after a quiet rest in the cool bus, I told her. The driver got me a drink of water, and I sipped it slowly, trying to ignore the tightness in my chest.

As I calmed down, I realized that the evil I had sensed was strong, but that there was something else about this place that was stronger. Fearfully at first, I opened my mind to the feeling as I gazed at the lovely house through the bus window. After a moment, I realized that the feeling was joy.

Taliesin lay dreaming on the brow of the hill where she had been built three times by a man who loved her very much. A terrible tragedy had taken place here, but afterward had come healing and new love, and creativity and joy. I relaxed. Any ghosts who lingered here now were happy ones. The vision I had seen was of one strong, isolated event that was powerful enough to affect a psychic with my retrocognitive abilities, but not to haunt the place permanently. For this, I was truly grateful.

Ellen and the others returned to the bus, and we drove back to the Visitor's Center. Ellen, still worried by my fainting spell, insisted that we sit down in the restaurant and eat a late lunch. The food brought color back to my cheeks, and after a short visit to the gift shop, we went back to my house—with Ellen driving, so I could rest.

That night, after Ellen was asleep, I took out the biography of Wright that I'd purchased to search for a section about the first fire at Taliesin—the one the guide had mentioned. After locating the right section, I skimmed back a few pages and read the story from the beginning.

Apparently, Wright had designed a house for a man in Oak Park, Illinois, and in the process had fallen in love with the man's wife, Martha, affectionately called "Mamah." The two wished to marry, but their spouses were against divorce, so they eloped to Europe.

The scandal this caused virtually destroyed Wright's architectural practice. Eventually, Mamah got her divorce, but Wright did not. Nonetheless, he returned to the United States to build a new home for himself and Mamah—the first Taliesin.

Mamah and her children lived there with Wright, and the two were very happy together. Then, while Wright was in Chicago finishing a project, a male servant recently discharged by Mamah returned to the house with a torch and an axe, set fire to Taliesin, and murdered nearly everyone staying in the house as the fire burned around them. Among those killed were Mamah and her two children. Only two people survived the mayhem.

I read on until almost dawn, amazed at how Wright had rebuilt both Taliesin and his life, finding happiness with his third wife, Olga, and maintaining a demanding and successful career until his death in 1959. I finally put the book down and turned out the light, at peace now with the vision I had seen at Taliesin. But as I drifted to sleep, one final thought crossed my mind: "I don't think I'll visit there again. Once was enough."

21

Cursed!

This story, *mon ami,* begins and ends with a curse. *Oui,* a curse! The hero of our story is the great *voyageur,* René-Robert Cavelier, Sieur de La Salle, who was born in Rouen, France, in 1643. As a young lad, La Salle joined the church, wishing to devote himself to *Le Bon Signeur.* But La Salle, already he was cursed with the wanderlust that would drive him all of his days. Unable to settle into a life of good works and piety, he quit the church and made his way to his brother's home in New France, hoping to be the first to find the northwest route to China.

The New World sparked a fire within La Salle. He settled onto one of the *seigneuries*—a plot of land granted to him by His Majesty King Louis XIV—and cultivated the friendship of the Iroquois who live nearby. Soon, he could speak the language fluently. Eagerly La Salle questioned them regarding the waterways in this New World. They spoke to him of mighty rivers to the west—those we call the Ohio and the Mississippi. The wanderlust burned within him when he heard of the great waters, for he believed they would take him through the wide lands to the Pacific, and from there to the Orient.

So La Salle, he abandoned his *seigneurie* as he had abandoned the church, and used the money he gained from the sale of his lands to finance an expedition. Setting off with fifteen men in five canoes, he made his way from Montreal to the Ohio River. The men explored along the Ohio as far as present-day Kentucky but turned back before reaching the Mississippi.

The wanderlust that cursed La Salle's heart, she abated for a time after this first trip. La Salle turned his energies to the construction of Fort Frontenac on *Lac Ontario,* which was used as a base for the very lucrative fur trade. King Louis, he was delighted with the success of the fort, and he granted La Salle a title and a large fur trade concession as a reward. And so La Salle settled down to enjoy life in the fort. He was happy for a time, *oui,* until the wanderlust struck harder than ever.

After six years, La Salle amassed enough money to build a *grand* sailing vessel in Cayuga Creek, which flows into the Niagara River below the mighty falls. *Le Griffon,* she was sixty feet long and weighed forty-five tons. The barque bore the name of a mythical beast with the head and wings of an eagle and the body of a lion, and she carried five large guns on her. *Le Griffon* was the largest ship to grace the waters of the Great Lakes at that time. With her, La Salle planned to explore the Great Lakes, seeking—always seeking—a path to China.

Unbeknownst to *le grand voyageur,* his ship did not meet with the approval of one Metiomek, a prophet of the Iroquois people. *Mais non.* Metiomek saw *Le Griffon* as an offense against the Great Spirit. He claimed that the size and grandeur of such a ship—previously unknown in those parts—made a mockery of the natural world and turned men's hearts away from the true path set out by the Great Spirit at the beginning of time. And so he put a curse on *Le Griffon*, the most powerful of curses that came in two parts: First the prophet stated that the once-mighty ship, she would become a shadow, traveling across the waters forever but never able to return to her home port. In the second part of the curse, he commanded the spirits of all those who sailed on her to share the same fate.

There was no sign that such a terrible curse lay upon the ship the day the explorers set forth to sail the Great Lakes. The weather was fair as La Salle and his men traveled across *Lac Erie*, *Lac Huron*, and *Lac Michigan*, landing finally in Green Bay. There, the crew members set to work amassing beaver pelts, for La Salle owed much money to his creditors. Once the hold was full, all but six members of the crew left with La Salle to explore the Saint Joseph River, seeking to find the mighty Mississippi River of which they had heard many tales. The six men who remained with the ship were instructed to take the cargo back to Niagara, discharge La Salle's debts, and return to Green Bay with enough lumber to build a second ship to be used in La Salle's explorations of the Mississippi.

Le Griffon, she set sail for Niagara under the command of her pilot, Luke the Dane, a massive man of uncertain temperament who stood seven feet tall in his stocking feet. And then the ship disappeared. Some say that she was caught in a storm and sank to the bottom of Lake Michigan. Others—including La Salle himself—believed that the crew mutinied, stole the rich cargo of fur pelts, and scuttled the ship. Whatever the true story may have been, *Le Griffon* was gone, and no one ever found the wrecked ship or her crew. The first part of Metiomek's curse had been fulfilled.

The loss of *Le Griffon* did not deter the mighty La Salle for long. In 1682, he led an expedition of forty men down the

CURSED!

Mississippi River to its basin, which he claimed for New France and named *La Louisiane* in honor of Louis XIV and his wife Anne. He then returned to France to persuade the king to start a new French colony on the Gulf of Mexico. In 1684, La Salle brought four ships and three hundred colonists with him from France to the New World. The expedition soon went awry. One ship was lost to pirates, and another went aground when La Salle missed the mouth of the Mississippi and landed his colonists at Matagorda Bay on the Texas coast on February 20, 1685. There, the colonists built Fort St. Louis, and La Salle set off to try and establish their exact location. He did not locate the Mississippi on his first trip, and on his second journey eastward, his disenchanted followers mutinied. La Salle was slain by Pierre Duhaut on March 19, 1687. And so the wanderlust that drove *le voyageur* in life led eventually to his death.

And what of the second part of Metiomek's curse? They say, *mon ami*, that *Le Griffon* still sails the Great Lakes, a ghost ship who will never reach her destination. She is manned by that fateful crew who first sailed with her, their souls slipping one by one back to her phantom decks after death. And so La Salle sails aboard his ship forever, and Great Lakes captains voyaging through Green Bay and the waters of northern Lake Michigan sometimes still see *Le Griffon* struggling against the stormy waves in a vain effort to find her way home. But she never will.

22

Bear-Walker

I was mixing up some cake batter at the kitchen counter when I glanced out the window and saw a black bear nosing around Old Lady Whitefeather's place. I watched it for a moment then turned back to my baking. I added a few spices to the batter, tasted it, and kept mixing. When I looked up again, the bear had reached the copse of trees at the edge of the Whitefeather property. Instead of retreating into the cool shelter out of the sweltering summer heat, it turned back to look at the house. Then it drew its mouth back into a snarl, and for a moment, flames flickered from its lips.

I dropped the wooden spoon I was using, and it sank deep into the batter until only the tip showed above the surface. I clutched my heart, which had grown so tight that pains were shooting all through my chest and abdomen. Bear-walker! It could be nothing else. Outside, the shape-shifter-turned-bear nosed its way into the thicket and disappeared.

Abandoning my cake, I went running through the house to find my husband. "Jim! Jimmy!" I shouted, almost knocking him over as he shot up the cellar steps and into the hallway, alarmed by my tone.

I caught desperately at his arm. "I just saw a bear-walker outside of Old Lady Whitefeather's house."

Jimmy's tanned face grew grim and lost its laugh lines as I described what I'd seen.

"We'd better tell Thomas," he said. "Well-spotted, love," he added, flicking his fingers tenderly across my cheek.

Thomas Whitefeather was the old lady's grandson, and her closest relative living nearby. Thomas and his wife Sheila lived right next door to us, directly across from his grandmother's place, and they were our best friends in the whole world. Our kids had grown up together, and we all kept a surreptitious eye on the spunky old *Anishinabe* grandmother who still told the old stories of her people and wanted to stay in her own home as long as she was able.

Jimmy went next door to talk to Thomas, who was painting an old shed in his backyard. I called Sheila, and we talked the matter over while I fished the wooden spoon out of my batter and finished mixing my cake. The kitchen was filled with the delicious smell of the baking cake when the two men came inside, still talking about the bear-walker.

"We'll have to wait and see if a light shows up, I guess," said Thomas, dropping a kiss on his wife's dark, silver-flecked hair and sitting down at the table beside her. A ball of light always appears near the house of a bear-walker's victim, and it stays there every night until that person dies. "It's pretty alarming, though, eh, *Watseka*?" He took his wife's hand as he spoke.

I smiled a bit at the nickname Thomas used for his wife as I poured him a cup of tea, handed a second to Jimmy, and refreshed the cup in front of Sheila. *Watseka* meant "pretty woman" in Potawatomi. Thomas's father married a real nice

Potawatomi woman, and Thomas is completely bilingual, something you might not suspect until he comes out with the occasional word or phrase in his maternal tongue.

Thomas was right, though. It was alarming. A bear-walker was an evil person—a witch—who could bend others to their evil ways or make them sick. To see one nosing about Old Lady Whitefeather's house was not a good sign. Still, she had seemed perfectly healthy when I saw her earlier this morning hanging her wash on the clothesline. Perhaps the bear-walker was just passing the house on its way somewhere else. The shiver that ran down my spine betrayed my internal doubt, but I chose not to say anything else at the moment.

That night, a bright white ball of light appeared in the trees beside Old Lady Whitefeather's house. Jimmy saw it first, and he knew at once that the bear-walker had cursed Old Lady Whitefeather. He watched the light as he went to summon Thomas and saw it slowly circling the house several times before settling once again in the trees.

Thomas and Jimmy hurried over and found the old grandmother trembling from head to toe and vomiting up her dinner. They took her to the local hospital right away, though they knew that modern medicine wasn't going to help much. The staff stabilized her and sent her home with some medication. It didn't work.

We took turns sitting with her as her illness increased in intensity. She couldn't keep anything in her stomach, not even water, and she grew weaker each hour. She knew it was a bear-walker getting her and that visiting the hospital wouldn't help. But at the insistence of all four of us, she agreed to go back to the emergency room on the second evening, and Thomas

BEAR-WALKER

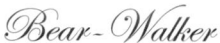

persuaded her to stay at the hospital when the doctor decided to admit her.

The truth was, we were all afraid to leave her in that house. Each night, the white ball of light shone in the trees, and if the bear-walker lore I'd learned as a child was true, on the fourth night, the creature would return to give the old lady more bad medicine. Anyone in the house with the intended victim would be paralyzed by the shape-shifter's magic during the entire visit and would remember nothing after it left. Four times the bear-walker would come, always on the fourth day. On the sixteenth day, the witch's victim would die.

I caught another glimpse of the black bear wandering the Whitefeather property at dusk on the fourth day. I rejoiced inwardly because there was no one there for the bear-walker to find. But when I dropped by the hospital on the morning of the fifth day of her illness, Old Lady Whitefeather patted my hand weakly and said: "That old Eliza Redroot was here last night. She's the one. She showed me the buckskin bag where she keeps a finger from each of her victims, and she told me my finger was next. Remember, she wanted to buy the house from me last year and I wouldn't sell? Now she's going to get it anyway. Tell Thomas to let her have it when I'm gone. I don't want her cursing anyone else."

I was stunned when I learned the bear-walker had followed Old Lady Whitefeather to the hospital, and I choked up at the idea of losing the little grandmother whom I love dearly. "We won't let her take you away," I said fiercely, stroking the silver hair back from her face. She smiled sadly, and I could see she didn't believe me.

Jimmy and I talked it over late into the night. Finally, he decided to take the next day off work and head up to the reservation at Lac du Flambeau and see if one of the elders could help us. We didn't say anything about it to Thomas and Sheila. We didn't want to raise false hope. But Jimmy came home at suppertime triumphant, with a small pouch of medicine for Old Lady Whitefeather. We hurried to the hospital and gave the medicine to her when the nurse was away. It didn't seem to make much of a difference at the time, but when we got home, the light was gone from the tree. And when Thomas and Sheila went to see her the next morning, the little grandmother had some color. By the end of the day, she was able to take fluids and even eat a little. The danger had passed.

Jimmy went to visit Eliza Redroot that evening. Jimmy had a message for the bear-walker from the elder on the reservation who had given him the cure. The message was for her ears only, so none of the rest of us ever knew exactly what it was. But it did the trick. Old Lady Whitefeather was soon back on her feet and puttering around her house and yard like always, and neither bear-walker nor light ever reappeared.

23

The Dark Horse

THE DELLS

It was dusk when Rikhard, my husband, ejected me kindly from Grandfather's sickroom, telling me to get some fresh air, eat, and take a rest. I'd been sitting up with the tiny, wrinkled old man all night and all day for nearly a week as his pneumonia grew worse. During the doctor's daily visit, he had warned us that Grandfather would probably not survive the night. I knew this even before he spoke. I had seen the gray look in my father-in-law's face and had seen his eyes searching vistas far beyond me, seeking the final passage across the river of death. I was saddened, but I knew that *Isoisä*—that's Finnish for "Grandfather"—was ready to go, and I did not wish him to remain in his feeble old body when a new one awaited him on the other side.

I staggered down the steep central staircase of our three-story farmhouse, holding tightly to the railing as a precaution against my shaking legs and tired, off-balance body. My daughter Tuuli met me at the bottom of the stairs—bless her heart—with a steaming-hot cup of coffee and guided me out onto the front porch with its spectacular view to gaze out over the rolling wooded hills as the summer night fell over the land. Unelma, my youngest daughter, trotted out with a plate full of food—*Karjalanpaisti* served with mashed potatoes, boiled swedes, and lingonberry purée—which she placed on a white wicker table beside my chair.

"Eat, Mama," she instructed firmly. "You must keep up your strength."

Behind her, Tuuli nodded solemnly. "We will sit with Papa and *Isoisä*," she added. "You rest."

I smiled at my lovely twin girls with their white-blonde hair and matching blue eyes. "*Kiitos,* girls," I said, thanking them gratefully and sagging deeper into the soft cushions of the white wicker chair. I listened as they climbed the stairs to the second floor, unable to lift the fork because I felt so tired and sad. So I rested, appreciating the scent of the food and watching the mist rising in the valley as I thought about my wonderful father-in-law.

Grandfather came to Wisconsin in 1909 with his wife and two little boys. They bought a farm in Bayfield County and worked very hard trying to make ends meet. But World War I put an end to that dream. Grandfather went overseas and was wounded. When he got back, his heart was no longer in farming. He moved down to Madison with his wife and sons and took a job as a laborer. After a few years—and two more sons—he was ready to try his hand at farming again. He bought a dairy farm near the Dells—this very one, in fact—and with hard work, made it a prosperous one. He even built a small cheese factory near the barn, and his wife became an expert cheese maker. They had two more sons—making a total of six—and their youngest became my husband and took over the family farm in due course. Grandfather had lived a very happy life and had loved living with our family once his lovely Anna died a few years back.

Absently, I picked up plate and fork and began eating the good meal my daughters had prepared. They adored their grandfather, and I was glad that he had spent so many of their formative years living in the house with us. I just wish they'd had the chance to know their spunky grandmother as well as they had come to know *Isoisä*.

As I chewed my mashed potatoes, I caught a glimpse of a tall rider atop a large, coal-black horse out of the corner of my eye. He was coming down the road toward the crossroads near our farm. In this age of the car and airplane, a horseman was a fairly rare sight. I turned to get a closer look and nearly choked on my potatoes. I could see the horse plainly now, cantering along the gravel at the side of the road, hardly visible in the growing darkness. But I no longer saw the rider!

This might not have been so strange, if the reins hadn't been gathered up tightly in an invisible hand, and the stirrups pointed out and down under the force of invisible boots. I shook my head to clear it, and with each shake, I saw the man flicker into and out of existence at the corner of my eye. So I narrowed them until I was squinting, and then I could see the rider again. He was tall with a grave, dark face and hollows under his fathomless eyes. He wore an old-fashioned black suit that made him look like an undertaker and a top hat that made him look like Abraham Lincoln.

The man dismounted at the crossroads, hitched his black horse to a tree beside the road, and came striding up the lane leading to our farmhouse at an incredible speed. Even with narrowed eyes, I could barely see him. But I could see the effect he had. The bushes and the underside of the trees writhed and bent as if under a massive blast of cold air. The grass at the

THE DARK HORSE

edge of the drive frosted over. And our dog Trixie ran and hid under the porch, whining all the way. I wanted to hide, too, but astonishment and fear kept me paralyzed as the flickering figure swept right up the porch past my wicker seat—blowing my hair right out of its bun—and into the house, stepping through the screen of the door without bothering to open it first.

Back at the road, the dark horse calmly began nibbling the grass at its feet as a fierce barking broke out from the neighbor's yard. They owned a big, mean bulldog—Zachariah—that brutalized all the other dogs in the area and had been known to bite. Zachariah raced out of his yard, roaring his anger at the trespasser on what he considered his turf. He leapt toward the horse, mouth open to bite. The horse's back leg lashed out so quickly I barely saw it, and then the dog was flying backward through the air. Zachariah landed with a terrible thump and lay for a second unmoving. Then he staggered to his feet, whimpered, and crawled away.

From the upstairs window, I heard my husband give a sudden cry of anguish. "Emilia," Rikhard shouted my name in alarm. "Emilia, come quickly to me!" Soft wails from the twins accompanied his call. The voices of my family woke me from my paralysis. I dropped my plate and fork on the small wicker table, wrenched open the screen door, and ran for the stairs. On the landing, I came face to face with the flickering, partially invisible man in the top hat. Death politely stepped aside for my rushing figure, doffing his hat as I passed. Beside him, the glowing figure of my father-in-law beamed upon me, his earthly sickness already forgotten. "*Hyvästi*, Emilia," Grandfather said in farewell. "Death's taking me up to heaven to be with my Anna! I'll see you soon."

I stopped in midrush and blinked in astonishment. On my second blink, both men were gone. But I heard the screen door to the porch creak a little, as if someone—or two someones—had just walked right through it without bothering to open it. Racing to the top of the steps, I looked out the front window in time to see the reins of the coal-black horse detached from the tree by a pair of invisible hands and a tall figure that I could barely see from the corner of my eye mount the horse. A moment later, I saw a small, wizened figure leap nimbly up behind Death and the dark horse ride off into the shadow of the trees and disappear. From the neighbor's house, I heard a terrified yip as the horse passed by. Zachariah went pelting for the house and crashed through the neighbor's screen door, breaking it to bits in his panic.

"Emilia," my husband called again, staggering to the door with tears running down his rugged face. "Grandfather is gone."

I ran to him and held him tight. A moment later, two pairs of arms surrounded both of us as the twins came over to comfort and be comforted. I wondered briefly if I should tell my family what I had just seen. But it would be too hard to explain. It would be enough, at least for now, to reassure them that *Isoisä* had gone to heaven. After all, I had his word on it, so I should know.

24

Deadly Hunter

The first sign of trouble came when Father tried to hire a native guide to take us deep into the northern woods of Wisconsin Territory the year after the Civil War ended to do some game hunting. It was just the three of us—Father, Jonathan, and me, Richard, the younger son. We lived in Chicago, and this trip was one of our very first ventures into the wilds of the American Frontier. It was by way of being a celebratory trip, since Jonathan had been taken into Father's very successful law practice as a junior member, and I had just graduated from a rather posh boarding school and been accepted into university.

I was just a gangling thing in those days, all long arms, long legs, awkward wrists, and floppy hair, who didn't look too promising. Nobody would have guessed, seeing me then, that I would top six-foot-six in my bare feet and have the brawny build of a lumberjack by the time I finished growing. In spite of my unprepossessing appearance and awkward ways back then, Father still graciously asked me to accompany him and Jonathan on the hunting trip.

Mother waved us off from our fancy Chicago home with tears in her eyes, fearful of what might happen to us in the terrible dark woods of the North Country. She'd heard stories all her life of fierce wolves and hungry bears, as well as dark spirits that would possess a man. Father just laughed at her. We would have a whole slew of native guides to accompany us on our trek to Lake Superior, and we would return triumphant, with more deer and bear meat than the family could eat in a year. But Mother wasn't so sure. She had a bad feeling about the trip, and she was frightened she would lose a member of her family to the evil denizens of the North County.

The first part of our trip was easy—sailing up the coast to the settlement. Folks there assured us that we would have no trouble hiring a few native tribesmen to guide us on our trip. And it was true that each man that Father approached listened to him eagerly for the first few minutes. Then his face would freeze partway through Father's speech, his mind pulling away from the conversation even though physically he did not move. And each conversation ended with a sharp negative shake of the head and with each potential guide walking away.

"What are you saying to them, Father?" asked Jonathan in that half-jovial, half-superior tone that I hated. Don't get me wrong, I do love my brother. But he was already as cynical a creature as ever walked the Earth, and vain to boot—though frankly, with his too-short frame, popped-out fish eyes, and slicked-back curly dark hair that perpetually shed white flakes of dandruff onto his shoulders, he really had no excuse for vanity.

"I don't understand it," Father said slowly. "Every time I tell the guides that we want to hunt up near Lake Superior, they break off negotiations. Tell me that the hunting is no good there and just walk away."

"The hunting, she *is* no good near the lake this year," a deep voice rumbled from behind us. A massive Potawatomi tribesman stepped out of the shadowy corner of the inn where we had repaired to eat our dinner and figure out what to do. "You should hunt somewhere else this season."

But Father had turned stubborn. First Mother and now this! He wanted to hunt up by Lake Superior. Two of his partners had gone hunting up there last season and had raved about it ever since. This was Father's first chance to go, and he was going to take it, even if it meant finding our way north without a guide.

The Potawatomi listened to his ranting in grave silence, dark eyes hooded against us. Now and then he asked a question or uttered a short sentence, and I was impressed by his clarity of thought, deftness of speech, and superior intelligence. If this man ever studied law, Father and Jonathan wouldn't stand a chance against him in court. But in this day and age, native tribesmen did not attend the white man's university or argue in his courts.

The Potawatomi's eyes were suddenly upon me, and we studied each other intently for a moment as Father raged, egged on unsubtly by Jonathan. Some sort of silent message passed between me and the tribesman, an acknowledgement of Father's stubbornness and Jonathan's vanity and the foolish pride of both that was sending us into danger. The fact was that nothing either of us said would change their minds. That moment of understanding sealed a lifelong friendship between me and the Potawatomi, who told us to call him Hawk.

The upshot of our conversation was that Hawk hired on to guide us north to hunt along the shores of Lake Superior. He brought along two other men to carry our equipment and keep camp for us: one was a French-Canadian trapper called Jean-Claude, and the other a wiry little Irish chap who gave his name as O'Toole. Nothing else. Just O'Toole. Together, the six of us headed north in the chill of autumn as the foliage grew brilliant and the birds began winging their way south. Jonathan tried to get Hawk to tell us why the other tribesmen were reluctant to make a potentially lucrative journey to the North Country, but Hawk wasn't talking.

We reached the shores of Lake Superior after a week of travel, canoeing the rivers and portaging across land. We had seen no one along the way. No lumber scouts. No settlers. No tribesmen. It was as if everyone in the North Country had fled the vicinity. The thought made me go cold. *Fled from what?* I wondered.

Hawk set up camp in a small clearing on the lakeshore, and soon we were gathered around the fire, eating beans and planning our first big hunt. Father and Jonathan talked excitedly about some bear tracks they had seen not far from our campsite and discussed various tracking methods with Jean-Claude. O'Toole—the expedition cook—hummed an Irish jig under his breath as he made another pot of coffee. The hunting talk didn't interest him. His duty was merely to stay in camp, catch fish, and prepare food and coffee at a moment's notice when we returned from a hard day's hunt.

On the far side of the fire, Hawk sat like a stone, dark eyes unfathomable. I watched the huge tribesman, who appeared to be sniffing the air, like a rabbit trying to scent the presence of a predator. The thought made me shiver. I accepted a mug of coffee from O'Toole and took a seat beside our guide.

"My mother says that dark spirits haunt the North Woods," I said softly, under cover of the lively conversation between my Father and Jean-Claude.

"Your mother is a wise woman," said Hawk, his tone equally low.

"Is something here with us?" I asked, my voice calm. In front of me, I watched the mug of coffee in my hands begin to tremble.

"I do not know," Hawk said reluctantly. "There have been rumors that something has come down from the far north. The elders of many tribes have seen it approaching in their dreams."

He broke off, staring into the fire.

"I myself have seen it," he said at last, his voice barely audible. "In a vision last summer."

I started, the hot coffee spilling out over my hand. I ignored the stinging sensation and whispered: "What have you seen?"

Hawk closed his eyes briefly, and his face grew grim.

"Wendigo," he whispered and then rose abruptly and walked off into the darkness.

Seeing his retreat, Jonathan smirked from the other side of the fire and said: "Don't scare off our native guide, little brother, unless you learned how to track bear at your boarding school."

"Knock it off, Jonathan," I said, rising and wiping my wet hand on my breeches. "I'm going to bed."

I crawled into the tent and settled down among the balsam boughs laid ready for the night, my mind churning. *Wendigo*, Hawk had said. What was a Wendigo? I'd never heard the term before, but the tone in which it was uttered had filled me with a nameless dread, and I was uncomfortably aware of being very far from civilization up here in the bleak splendor of the remote North Woods. I felt small and insignificant amid the beautiful, merciless forest with its massive trees and huge wild beasts. I stayed awake for a long time, trembling under the covers. It was only the familiar sound of my Father's bass voice singing some of the old French-Canadian *voyageur* songs with Jean-Claude that finally calmed my fears and lulled me to sleep.

I was awakened during the night by a loud sound in the tent. I froze, my heart pounding loudly against my rib cage, and held my breath, trying to identify the sound. Then my Father let out a second loud snore, and I let out my breath in a sigh of relief. I nudged him a little, and he turned over and settled down again, breathing softly now. Then I lay on my back, staring uneasily up at the dark roof of the tent, unable to get back to sleep. The night was unusually quiet. There was no sound save the soft whisper of the breeze. No night-owls called, no insects buzzed, no creatures stirred the underbrush. Within the primeval forest surrounding us was the silence of death.

As I lay there, I became aware of a sickly, almost sweet smell, like that of rotten fruit. I stiffened, remembering the way that Hawk had been sniffing the air. I drew the scent into my nose, body tense with fear, but already the smell was fading . . . fading . . . gone. After four or five minutes, I heard the tentative hooting of an owl followed by the croak of a frog, and then the rustle of little creatures in the underbrush. I relaxed and went back to sleep.

We woke early, ready to track bear in the dim light of dawn. We found the fire burnt down to coals, the food still tied up high in a tree, and O'Toole gone. Vanished into thin air. At first,

Father thought the Irishman was playing a joke on us. All his gear was still in the tent he shared with Jean-Claude, so he couldn't have gone far. We called and searched the surrounding forest. It was Hawk's keen eyes that spotted the barely perceptible footprints leading toward water's edge—and not back again.

For a moment, the only sound was the wash of little waves along the rocky lake shore. Then Father said: "Do you think he drowned himself? Why would he do that?"

Hawk didn't answer. He was looking at the grass, at the rocks, at the dirt. I wondered what his dark eyes saw there. I couldn't even see the cook's footprints when they were pointed out to me. Whatever Hawk saw on the ground made his mouth go grim, and the shadow of a known horror passed over his face. "We must leave here at once," he said suddenly, straightening to his massive height and staring down at my father. "He was not drowned. He was taken."

It was then I remembered the strange silence in the night and the sickeningly sweet odor I had smelled. I envisioned the cook stepping out of his tent into that silence to answer the call of nature. And being taken by . . . what? That was the question Father was asking. What had taken the cook? A bear? A cougar?

"Wendigo," said Hawk grimly and began packing up our gear.

When he heard the word *Wendigo,* Jean-Claude gasped and crossed himself. Glancing toward him, I saw that the tough old *voyageur* was shaken to the core. He peered this way and that into the woods, his brown eyes searching for something that obviously terrified him, breath coming in short, sharp gasps, face as pale as snow.

Then he too leapt forward and rapidly began dismantling the tent.

"Stop, man, stop!" roared my Father. "Why must we leave? What is this Wendigo? I paid good money for this trip. And I'm not leaving until we find O'Toole!"

I shivered with nerves. The French Canadian's terror was catching. Suddenly, I passionately wanted out of this place. Jean-Claude turned a face of livid terror toward Father. "You won't find O'Toole," he said fiercely. "Not if the Wendigo got him. You can stay here if you want. I'm leaving."

"We're all leaving," said Hawk, looming up behind Jonathan and making him start with fright. "Right now."

And we left, our gear mashed into packs and canoes any which way. Father and Jonathan were dancing with rage and irritation, but they followed the tall tribesman and the French Canadian because they had no choice. We could never find our way alone in this vast, untamed wilderness.

We portaged with the canoes more than two miles before striking the river. Just before we pushed off, Hawk spotted something in the brush. He stalked forward, disappeared into the trees, and returned with the torn body of O'Toole. The cook's head lolled on a broken neck, his ribs had been split apart, and his guts torn out. There were teeth marks covering his throat and one side of his broken body. It was obvious that he had been eaten by something big.

My Father's protests died away at the sight of the poor dead cook. We couldn't get him buried fast enough, and Father himself pushed off the canoes. It was only when we were rapidly traveling downstream, me and Jonathan and Jean-Claude in one boat and Hawk and Father in the other, that I ventured to ask Jean-Claude about the creature that had killed the cook.

"Yes, what *is* a Wendigo?" Jonathan added loudly. Too loudly. Jean-Claude glanced about wildly and hushed him. Jonathan repeated his question sotto voce. This time, the French Canadian answered him.

"Cannibal," he whispered as we paddled at top speed down the river. "Dark spirit of the woods with a craving for human flesh. The more the Wendigo eats, the more it craves. It is tall and gray-green like a rotting corpse, all cracked skin and clotted blood and pus. You smell them first—the sickly sweet odor of decay—and if they catch you, they eat you, like poor O'Toole." I gasped aloud when he described the smell, and he gave me a sympathetic smile, misunderstanding my fear. I had smelled the Wendigo last night. It had passed right beside my tent!

"Sometimes," Jean-Claude continued over the splash of the river, "a Wendigo will call a man by name. When it calls, you must obey. The Wendigo will run with you across the treetops, across the sky at blinding speed until you bleed beneath the eyes and your feet burn away to stumps. Then it drops you to the ground like a bird dropping a fish on a rock. Any man that runs with a Wendigo, becomes a Wendigo himself."

Regrettably, Jonathan—the hard-headed attorney—laughed when he heard this. "That's just nonsense," he said derisively. "It's obvious that O'Toole was eaten by a bear. Wendigo. Ha! Just a rural myth."

Jean-Claude clammed up after that and spoke not a word to either of us until we beached the canoes at dusk. Hawk wanted to keep going through the night, but Father insisted that we stop and rest. We had traveled many miles downriver during the day, and surely had left the beast that killed O'Toole far behind, Father argued. This would have been true enough if we were dealing with a living creature. But I wasn't as convinced as Jonathan was that we were. Wendigo—dark spirit of the North Country—the creature that my mother feared would kill her family. Was it only a myth? If not, then we were dealing with a creature that could fly through the air. To such a creature, what were a few miles?

I could see Hawk and Jean-Claude felt as I did. They left most of our belongings in the canoes, ready to launch out onto the river immediately if something happened. Then Jean-Claude set up two of the three tents while Hawk made a large fire and cooked a simple meal for us. Father and Jonathan—the two practical attorneys—sat on one side of the fire, talking in low tones about the superstitious nonsense that had ruined our hunting trip. I sat with Hawk and Jean-Claude on the other side. We ate in silence, listening to night settle over the forest around us. We were still five days from the nearest settlement, I thought, a tremor of fear shaking my body. Five days.

As soon as he finished eating, Jean-Claude fled into the tent to sleep, fear pulsing from his whipcord hard body. I am not sure what shelter a tent would provide from a determined Wendigo, but it seemed to offer comfort to the French-Canadian trapper. When he was gone, I said to Hawk: "Tell me about your vision. Did you see the Wendigo kill O'Toole?"

Hawk shook his dark head. "No, Richard," he said. "I saw myself . . . " he hesitated, staring into the fire.

"You saw yourself . . . " I prompted when the silence grew too long.

"I saw myself killing a Wendigo to save someone's life," he replied at length, avoiding my gaze. My eyes nearly popped out of my head.

"They can be killed?" I gasped. "How? I thought they were dark spirits?"

"A Wendigo has a heart made of ice and snow," said Hawk. "If you pierce that heart with an arrow of fire, the Wendigo is no more."

My eyes went to the bow and quiver of arrows that were always strapped to Hawk's side. I had wondered why he favored them over a gun. Now I knew.

We soon followed Jean-Claude's example and settled into the tents for the night. No one would be tempted to leave the shelter tonight for any reason. Not after what happened to O'Toole. Father placed himself in the center of the tent, between me and Jonathan, to protect us, I think. Anything coming through the door would get him first.

We lay awake a long time, pretending to sleep. I imagined Jean-Claude and Hawk lying awake in the next tent, listening . . . listening. Finally Jonathan started to snore, and Father after him. The familiar sound relaxed me, and I was nearly asleep when my nose was assailed by a sickeningly sweet scent. I sat bolt upright in terror. Wendigo! I wanted to shout for Hawk. But in that moment, a violent movement shook the tent. Father woke with a startled shout, and Jonathan rolled over, trembling with shock. From somewhere outside came a thunderous voice. It was close to the tent, but came from overhead rather than beside us. The volume of sound was immense and wild, full of an abominable power that was as sickly sweet as the smell of the demon. It called a man's name.

"Jon-a-thannnnnn."

And Jonathan was on his feet, leaping past Father, bumping into the tent pole, then plunging through the canvas door. He was running so fast his body seemed to blur in the dim firelight. As he ran, he was joined by an immensely tall gray-green figure. They disappeared into the trees before Father and I could draw a breath.

I think I screamed. I know Father did. We bumped into each other twice before we managed to scramble from the tent. "Jonathan," Father bellowed. "Johnny! Come back, son! Come back!"

He ran toward the woods in the direction taken by his elder son, but Hawk caught him and pulled him back.

"There's nothing you can do," the Potawatomi said. "The Wendigo has taken him."

"Let me go! I must find my son," screamed Father. It took all of the massive tribesman's strength to hold him back.

"What can you do in the dark, *mon ami?*" asked Jean-Claude, who stood trembling beside the fire, his face as white as a ghost. "At least wait until morning to look for him."

"Jonathan just panicked when the wind struck our tent," Father said defiantly. "That's all. There is no such thing as a Wendigo." He stared from one face to the other, and the grave compassion he saw there broke his defiance. "He will come back to camp. You'll see," he continued almost pleadingly. "And I'm staying right here until he returns. I will not leave here without my son!"

"We did not ask you to leave," said Hawk, laying a massive hand on Father's shoulder.

And then, from somewhere high above us, we heard a terrible cry. "Oh! Oh! My feet of fire! My burning feet of fire!" It was Jonathan's voice. Father gasped and dropped to his knees, as somewhere above the trees, Jonathan shrieked: "Oh! Oh! This height and fiery speed!"

A terrible rush of wind whipped the treetops, as if a storm were approaching. Then all was silence, and the stench of decay slowly faded from the riverbank. Father, his face gray with pain, looked up into Hawk's dark eyes. "I will not leave without my son," he repeated. The Potawatomi nodded his understanding, his eyes brimming with sorrow.

We sat by the fire, silently waiting through the long hours for dawn to come. None of us spoke. What could we say? We had all heard that horrified wail. But there was nothing we could do to help Jonathan during the long darkness of night.

I dozed a couple of times, leaning against my grief-stricken Father for comfort. Toward dawn, I was awakened by the sound of a rushing wind. Something dropped heavily through the trees beside the river. In the dim gray light, I felt Father stiffen beside me and saw Hawk leapt to his feet, bow in one hand and arrow in the other. The tip of the arrow was wrapped in cloth, and he pushed it into the fire as I sat up, rubbing my eyes.

Then I saw him. Jonathan came lurching toward us through the half-light, his step faltering, uncertain. At least, I think it was Jonathan, though it seemed a ghastly caricature of the brother I had known all my life. The face was twisted, features drawn about into strange and terrible proportions, skin loose and hanging, as though Jonathan had been subjected to extraordinary air pressures and tensions. The skin below his eyes was red with blood, and his feet were blackened stumps. My nose caught the penetrating odor of rotten fruit as my brother lurched toward the clearing, his eyes fixed on Father.

There was something about the look in his eyes . . .

I didn't think; I just reacted, shoving myself in front of Father as Jonathan suddenly sprang forward with supernatural

DEADLY HUNTER

speed, his mouth a gaping black hole as he screamed in hunger and fury. There were claws at the ends of his hands, curved and vicious, and his eyes burned as he slashed out at me, intent on the kill. Then a fiery arrow winged its way over my shoulder from Hawk's bow. It caught Jonathan in the chest, penetrating his icy heart, stopping him a mere two feet from my body. He fell to the ground, momentum sliding him forward until he reached my feet. He screamed in agony, and gray-green smoke billowed out of his mouth and rose to the treetops.

Behind me, Hawk sent another flaming arrow up toward the swirling gray-green mist that was forming into a tall man-shaped figure that looked like a rotting corpse, all cracked skin and clotted blood and pus. The Wendigo rose with a terrific rushing noise that whipped the trees with hurricane force. But the flaming arrow rose faster, smashing right through the center of the Wendigo. It screamed and exploded into flames. At my feet, Jonathan's body also burst into flames. Jean-Claude and Father pulled me backward, away from the danger, as my brother and the Wendigo burned to death before my eyes.

We carried what was left of Jonathan back to the settlement wrapped in a deerskin that the trapper gave us from his pack. Father wanted to bury him in the family plot in Chicago. Although we never spoke of it, I realized that in his vision, Hawk had seen himself shooting Jonathan to save my life. That was why he had accompanied us to the North Country when no other tribesman would go. Jean-Claude left us as soon as we reached the settlement, glad to be rid of us and the terrible memory of that aborted hunting trip. But the Potawatomi tribesman accompanied us to our ship and bade us farewell. Father tried to press money on him in thanks for saving my life, but Hawk would not accept it. It was enough for him to know that he was sending two of Mother's menfolk back home to her, when she could so easily have lost us all.

Father never went hunting again. He lost his heart for it after our terrible trip. But not me. Every year, on the anniversary of Jonathan's death, Hawk and I take a hunting trip up north, and I visit the small cross we had erected on the riverbank where Jonathan died and Hawk defeated the Wendigo.

25

North

In the end, they ran north. It was all they could do. The enemy warriors were pouring into the land with terrible force, killing any who stood in their way. Even killing those who didn't. Death was the only option they gave, and as the stories of their crimes grew, so did the panic. And so the family fled; the warrior and his wife and their three little children. They were not alone. Many others joined them as they ran north. To get away from the invaders was the only thought in the communal mind. Away.

They traveled up the peninsula at speed. As they ran, a troubled thought plagued the warrior's mind: *What would they do when they reached the top of the peninsula? They could retreat to the island, perhaps. But what if the enemy followed? The enemy always followed.*

They ran all day, all night, carrying the children when they grew too tired to run. It was on the third day, as they neared the top of the peninsula, that they heard harsh cries in front of them. Another tribesman, fleeing with his family, had brushed aside a strangely clad, crippled old woman who was hobbling down the path toward them, begging for food.

"Away, old woman. Do not bother us now," shouted the battle-scarred tribesman, snatching his youngest child out of the beggar-woman's reach and knocking her to the ground. The warrior sprang forward at once to glare at the bully, war club in hand. "How dare you turn on the aged?" he shouted. "Too soon, we will be old ourselves. Would you have others treat you in the fashion you have treated this old woman today?" For a moment, the two men glared at one another. Then shame claimed the battle-scarred man. He looked away, snapped an order at his worn-out wife, and pulled his family back into a northward run.

The warrior turned and found his lovely wife helping the crooked old woman to her feet. "It is not safe here, mother," she said, her lovely brown eyes filled with compassion. "The enemy comes, hard on our heels. You must flee with us. Our children have no grandmother, and it would please us if you would consent to fill that role in our family." The warrior beamed with pride. His bride, the joy of his heart. The children had surrounded the old woman, patting her arms and back, calling her Grandmother. There were tears in the crippled woman's eyes as she consented to join them. "You will not regret your kindness to me," she told the warrior and his wife.

They slowed their pace a little to accommodate her hobble and fed her from their dwindling supplies. There would be time later, when they reached the island, to hunt and fish. Now they must run. Finally, the warrior swept up the old woman's frail frame into his strong arms and ran on, carrying her and his youngest child while his wife helped the older children along.

The shores of the passage were crowded with fleeing families. There were no canoes to spare, and none who had already reached the relative safety of the island wished to make the journey back to the peninsula.

"Do not fear. I will make us a canoe," the warrior told his family with sinking heart. Too long. It would take too long. The reports told of the enemy only a day away.

"We could float across on logs," his wife said, eyeing the old woman and children dubiously.

It was then that the crooked old crone proved her worth. "No need, daughter," she said. "I have a canoe hidden not far from this place. Come."

Taking the two older children by the hand, she led them along the shore until they reached a place where the trees grew right up to water's edge. There she showed them a hidden cache full of dried meat, blankets, medicinal herbs, and a canoe just large enough for one family. The warrior's wife embraced the crippled old lady in joyful thanks for their rescue. Within a very few minutes, they were inside the canoe and navigating the tricky passageway between peninsula and the island refuge.

They were welcomed by the warrior's cousin and many other members of their tribe who had made the difficult journey north. They set up temporary housekeeping in a clearing with two other families. The warrior immediately joined the men, who were making weapons for the invasion that would surely be upon them in just a few days. They worked as men without hope, knowing that the enemy was far stronger than they; that in the end, their efforts would make no difference. But they would die bravely— all of them. Even the women and children would fight in the end, rather than submit to the brutal murderers who pursued them.

Within two days, the north shore of the peninsula was lined with the camp of the enemy. Many were the warriors standing

NORTH

on the banks; many were the canoes that lined the shore. They could hear the sound of distant chanting, see figures dancing ecstatically around the war fires that night. Battle would come in the morning. Death would come in the morning.

The warrior spent that night with his family. None of them slept. They huddled together for the last time, holding each other and listening to the war chant floating over the passage. Just before dawn, the warrior gave each of his children and his wife the knives he had been saving for such a moment as this. *Better to die fighting* was the unspoken message he sent them as he ceremoniously handed out the weapons. He hesitated when he reached the old grandmother, already a dear member of the family. He had no knife for her. She had not been with the family at the time he crafted the weapons.

"I need no weapon, my son," the old lady said with a smile. She rose to her feet, and she seemed taller, straighter than she had before. Her face looked younger. She pulled his face down, kissed his forehead. Then she kissed each one of the children and hugged his wife, murmuring a blessing upon her.

"Come, my son," she said, and beckoned the warrior out into the dim light of predawn. Baffled by her sudden transformation, the warrior followed. With each step she took, the woman grew straighter, taller, younger, and more beautiful. One by one, they were joined by the other men as they took leave of their families and headed to the shore, there to intercept and fight off the invaders as long as they could. Strangely, the warrior was the only one who appeared to notice the woman in their midst. To the other men, she was invisible.

By this time, the chanting had stopped on the far shore, and the warrior knew the enemy was preparing to cross the passage.

He stopped at water's edge beside the old grandmother—who now looked as young and lovely as his bride—and she turned to him, saying: "For your kindness to a crippled old woman, I shall call on the power of the dead in this passage to make an end to the enemies who plague you."

Across the water, the first of the enemy canoes launched into the passage. Behind him, the warrior felt the men tense, heard the sharp, indrawn breaths. Out of the corner of his eye, he saw war clubs raised, arrows notched, spears flourished. But his gaze was fixed on the woman whom he called grandmother as she raised her arms and began to chant in a language he had never heard, her body growing translucent and filling with light.

Oblivious to her presence, the grim-faced men of his tribe prepared for battle. As the enemy canoes reached the halfway mark between peninsula and island, a breeze sprang up out of nowhere, lashing the trees. Out in the passage, the water grew choppy. The enemy canoes were tossed about. And then the water began to swirl at the center, slowly at first. Almost unnoticeably. Then faster, harder, deeper. A giant whirlpool opened in the center of the passage, sweeping the enemy canoes into its depths. The men on the island shouted in surprise, but their voices were lost in the screams and wails of terror as more and more of the enemy canoes were caught in the inexorable grip of the whirlpool. Around and around they were swept, reaching lower and lower, down to the bubbling maelstrom at the center. Those of the enemy still on the shore dropped their weapons and fled in terror at the sight.

It could have been moments, or hours, that the vortex churned. The warrior never knew how much time had elapsed when suddenly, the whirlpool collapsed in on itself, burying the enemy in its depths, never to rise again. A few broken pieces of canoe bubbled to the surface, the only sign that anyone had tried to cross the passage that morning.

Around him, the men of his tribe gave a great shout of incredulous joy, leaping and dancing and pounding each other on the backs. Others called out their thanks to the spirit that had saved them. The warrior stood very still and looked at the spirit woman, who was invisible to all save him.

"This island shall be a place of refuge for the pure in heart," she told the warrior as the last of the glow faded from her body. "When evil forces threaten those living in the North, all who seek the safety of the island will be saved, for the passage is protected by the spirits of the dead. Remember this, and take courage."

As she uttered the last word, the woman vanished without a trace. A moment later the warrior was caught in an embrace by his young cousin and pulled back to the makeshift village to celebrate the miracle that had saved the tribe from its enemies. In that moment, the warrior vowed to live on the island all his days under the watchful eye of the spirit who had saved his people. His family would stay in the North.

Resources

Adams, Peter. *Early Loggers and the Sawmill*. St. Catharines, Ontario: Crabtree Publishing Company, 1981.

Apps, Jerry. *Ringlingville USA*. Madison: Wisconsin Historical Society Press, 2005.

———. *Tents, Tigers, and the Ringling Brothers*. Madison: Wisconsin Historical Society Press, 2007.

Asala, Joanne. *Norwegian Troll Tales*. Iowa City, Iowa: Penfield Books, 1994.

Asfar, Dan, and Edrick Thay. *Ghost Stories of America*. Edmonton, Alberta: Ghost House Books, 2001.

Battle, Kemp P. *Great American Folklore*. New York: Doubleday & Company, Inc., 1986.

Bishop, Hugh E. *Haunted Lake Superior*. Duluth, Minn.: Lake Superior Port Cities Inc., 2003.

Botkin, B. A., ed. *A Treasury of American Folklore*. New York: Crown, 1944.

———. *A Treasury of Mississippi Folklore*. New York: Crown, 1955.

———. *A Treasury of Railroad Folklore*. New York: Crown, 1953.

Boyer, Dennis. *Driftless Spirits*. Madison, Wis.: Prairie Oak Press, 1996.

———. *Giants in the Land: Folk Tales & Legends of Wisconsin*. Madison, Wis.: Prairie Oak Press, 2000.

———. *Gone Missing!* Oregon, Wis.: Badger Books Inc, 2002.

———. *Hilltales from Vernon County*. Dodgeville, Wis.: Eagletree Press, 1995.

———. *Iowa County Folktales*. Dodgeville, Wis.: Eagletree Press, 1994.

———. *Northern Frights!* Oregon, Wis.: Badger Books Inc., 1998.

Brewer, J. Mason. *American Negro Folklore*. Chicago: Quadrangle Books, 1972.

Brown, Charles E. *Bluenose Brainerd Stories.* Madison: Wisconsin Historical Society, 1943. Online facsimile at www.wisconsinhistory .org/turningpoints/search.asp?id=1622; visited on May 1, 2007.

————. *Brimstone Bill.* Madison: Wisconsin Historical Society, 1942. Online facsimile at www.wisconsinhistory.org/turningpoints/search .asp?id=1622; visited on May 1, 2007.

————. *Johnny Inkslinger.* Madison: Wisconsin Historical Society, 1944. Online facsimile at www.wisconsinhistory.org/turningpoints/ search.asp?id=1622; visited on May 1, 2007.

————. *Ghost Tales.* Madison: Wisconsin Historical Society, 1931. Online facsimile at www.wisconsinhistory.org/turningpoints/search .asp?id=1622; visited on May 1, 2007.

————. *Paul Bunyan Tales.* Madison: Wisconsin Historical Society, 1922. Online facsimile at www.wisconsinhistory.org/turningpoints/ search.asp?id=1622; visited on May 1, 2007.

————. *Whiskey Jack Yarns.* Madison: Wisconsin Historical Society, 1940. Online facsimile at www.wisconsinhistory.org/turningpoints/ search.asp?id=1622; visited on May 1, 2007.

Brown, Dorothy Moulding. *Wisconsin Circus Lore, 1850–1908: Stories of the Big Top, Sawdust Ring, Menagerie, and Sideshows.* Madison: Wisconsin Folklore 1947. Online facsimile at www.wisconsinhistory .org/turningpoints/search.asp?id=1229; visited on July 1, 2007.

Brunvand, Jan Harold. *The Choking Doberman and Other Urban Legends.* New York: W. W. Norton, 1984.

————. *The Vanishing Hitchhiker.* New York: W. W. Norton, 1981.

Buckley, J. A. *Cornish Mining—Underground.* Redruth, Cornwall: Tor Mark, 1989.

Coffin, Tristram P., and Hennig Cohen, eds. *Folklore from the Working Folk of America.* New York: Doubleday, 1973.

————. *Folklore in America.* New York: Doubleday & AMP, 1966.

Cohen, Daniel. *Ghostly Tales of Love & Revenge.* New York: Andrew Publishing Group, 1992.

Cohen, Daniel, and Susan Cohen. *Hauntings & Horrors.* New York: Dutton Children's Books, 2002.

Copeland, Louis Albert. *Cornish in Southwest Wisconsin: Excerpt from Collections of the State Historical Society of Wisconsin, Volume XIV, 1898.* Mineral Point: Southwest Wisconsin Cornish Society, 2001.

Dorson, R. M. *America in Legend.* New York: Pantheon Books, 1973.

———. *Bloodstoppers & Bearwalkers.* Cambridge, Mass.: Harvard University Press, 1952.

Editors of Life. *The Life Treasury of American Folklore.* New York: Time Inc., 1961.

Erdoes, Richard, and Alfonso Ortiz. *American Indian Myths and Legends.* New York: Pantheon Books, 1984.

Fapso, Richard J. *Norwegians in Wisconsin.* Madison: The Wisconsin Historical Society Press, 2001.

Flanagan, J. T., and A. P. Hudson. *The American Folk Reader.* New York: A. S. Barnes & Co., 1958.

Godfrey, Linda S., and Richard D. Hendricks. *Weird Wisconsin.* New York: Sterling Publishing Co., Inc., 2005.

Hale, Frederick. *The Swiss in Wisconsin.* Madison: The State Historical Society of Wisconsin, 1994.

Leach, M. *The Rainbow Book of American Folk Tales and Legends.* New York: The World Publishing Co., 1958.

Leary, James P. *Wisconsin Folklore.* Madison: University of Wisconsin Press, 1998.

Leeming, David, and Jake Page. *Myths, Legends, & Folktales of America.* New York: Oxford University Press, 1999.

Levy, Hannah Heidi, and Brian G. Borton. *Famous Wisconsin Ghosts and Ghost Hunters.* Oregon, Wis.: Badger Books Inc., 2005.

Lewis, Chad, and Terry Fisk. *The Wisconsin Road Guide to Haunted Locations.* Eau Claire, Wis.: Unexplained Research Publishing Company, 2004.

Long, Megan. *Ghosts of the Great Lakes.* Toronto, Ontario: Lynx Images, Inc., 2003.

Matson, Elizabeth, and Stuart Stotts. *The Bookcase Ghost.* Shorewood, Wis.: Midwest Traditions, 1996.

McSherry, Jr., Frank D., Charles G. Waugh, and Martin H. Greenberg, eds. *Ghosts of the Heartland.* Nashville, Tenn.: Rutledge Hill Press, 1990.

Mott, A. S. *Ghost Stories of America, Volume II.* Edmonton, Alberta: Ghost House Books, 2003.

———. *Ghost Stories of Wisconsin.* Auburn, Wis.: Lone Pine Publishing International, 2006.

Norman, Michael, and Beth Scott. *Historic Haunted America.* New York: Tor Books, 1995.

Peck, Catherine, ed. *A Treasury of North American Folk Tales.* New York: W. W. Norton, 1998.

Pohlen, Jerome. *Oddball Wisconsin.* Chicago: Chicago Review Press, 2001.

Polley, J., ed. *American Folklore and Legend.* New York: Reader's Digest Association, 1978.

Rath, Jay. *The W-Files: True Reports of Wisconsin's Unexplained Phenomena.* Black Earth, Wis.: Trails Books, 1997.

Rider, Geri. *Ghosts of Door County.* Wever, Iowa: Quixote Press, 1992.

Rosebrough, Amy, and Bobbie Malone. *Water Panthers, Bears, and Thunderbirds: Exploring Wisconsin's Effigy Mounds.* Madison: Wisconsin Historical Society Press, 2003.

Russell, John. *Wiscomical.* Menomonie, Wis.: Oak Point Press, 2003.

Russell, Lou, and John Russell. *Wisconsin Lore and Legends.* Menomonie, Wis.: Oak Point Press, 1989.

Schwartz, Alvin. *Scary Stories to Tell in the Dark.* New York: Harper Collins, 1981.

Scott, Beth, and Michael Norman. *Haunted Heartland.* New York: Warner Books, 1985.

———. *Haunted Wisconsin.* Black Earth, Wis.: Trails Books, 2001.

Skinner, Charles M. *American Myths and Legends, Vol. 1.* Philadelphia: J. B. Lippincott, 1903.

Smith, David Lee. *Folklore of the Winnebago Tribe.* Norman: University of Oklahoma Press, 1997.

Spence, Lewis. *North American Indians: Myths and Legends Series.* London: Bracken Books, 1985.

Stonehouse, Frederick. *Haunted Lake Michigan.* Duluth, Minn.: Lake Superior Port Cities, Inc., 2006.

———. *Haunted Lakes.* Duluth, Minn.: Lake Superior Port Cities, Inc., 1997.

———. *Haunted Lakes II.* Duluth, Minn.: Lake Superior Port Cities, Inc., 2000.

Wyman, Walker D. *Wisconsin Folklore.* River Falls: University of Wisconsin, 1979.

Zeitlin, Steven J., Amy J. Kotkin, and Holly Cutting Baker. *A Celebration of American Family Folklore.* New York: Pantheon Books, 1982.

About the Author

S. E. Schlosser has been telling stories since she was a child, when games of "let's pretend" quickly built themselves into full-length tales acted out with friends. A graduate of Houghton College, the Institute of Children's Literature, and Rutgers University, she created and maintains the award-winning Web site Americanfolklore.net, where she shares a wealth of stories from all fifty states, some dating back to the origins of America. Sandy spends much of her time answering questions from visitors to the site. Many of her favorite e-mails come from other folklorists who delight in practicing the old tradition of who can tell the tallest tale.

About the Illustrator

Artist Paul Hoffman trained in painting and printmaking, with his first extensive illustration work on assignment in Egypt, drawing ancient wall reliefs for the University of Chicago. His work graces books of many genres—children's titles, textbooks, short story collections, natural history volumes, and numerous cookbooks. For *Spooky Wisconsin*, he employed a scratchboard technique and an active imagination.

Also in the Spooky Series by S. E. Schlosser
and Paul G. Hoffman:

Spooky California

Spooky Campfire Tales

Spooky Canada

Spooky Maryland

Spooky Massachusetts

Spooky Michigan

Spooky New England

Spooky New Jersey

Spooky New York

Spooky Pennsylvania

Spooky South

Spooky Southwest

Spooky Texas